REFLECTIONS ON
DALLAS WILLARD'S
TEACHING ON FAITH
& FORMATION

ETERNAL LIVING

Edited by Gary W. Moon

IVP Books

An imprint of InterVarsity Press
Downers Grove, Illinois

InterVarsity Press
P.O. Box 1400, Downers Grove, IL 60515-1426
www.ivpress.com
email@ivpress.com

InterVarsity Press® is the book-publishing division of InterVarsity Christian Fellowship/USA®, a movement of students and faculty active on campus at hundreds of universities, colleges and schools of nursing in the United States of America, and a member movement of the International Fellowship of Evangelical Students. For information about local and regional activities, write Public Relations Dept., InterVarsity Christian Fellowship/USA, 6400 Schroeder Rd., P.O. Box 7895, Madison, WI 53707-7895, or visit the IVCF website at www.intervarsity.org.

While all stories in this book are true, some names and identifying information in this book have been changed to protect the privacy of the individuals involved.

Cover design: Cindy Kiple
Interior design: Beth McGill
Images: Dallas Willard and his wife: Dieter Zander
　　　　Dallas Willard: Courtesy of InterVarsity Christian Fellowship/USA
　　　　Dallas Willard (from a graduation): Brad Elliott/Westmont

ISBN 978-0-8308-3595-9 (print)
ISBN 978-0-8308-9708-7 (digital)

Printed in the United States of America ∞

Library of Congress Cataloging-in-Publication Data
Eternal living : reflections on Dallas Willard's teaching on faith and formation / edited by Gary W. Moon.
　　pages cm
　ISBN 978-0-8308-3595-9 (hardcover : alk. paper)
　1. Willard, Dallas, 1935-2013. I. Moon, Gary W., 1956–
　BX4827.W47E84 2014
　230.092--dc23

2014039075

P 25　24　23　22　21　20　19　18　17　16　15　14　13　12　11　10　9　8　7　6　5　4　3　2　1
Y 35　34　33　32　31　30　29　28　27　26　25　24　23　22　21　20　19　18　17　16　15

This book is dedicated to

Dallas Albert Willard—
there were indeed giants in the land.

Bertha Von Allman Willard—
she lovingly stepped into the shoes of Maymie Willard
after her premature death and later said of Dallas,
"We were so young, we had to raise each other."

To Dallas Willard's family, friends, colleagues and students,
the thirty who contributed to the this book and
the thousands more who could have.

Contents

Preface 11

Introduction: Living in the Glow of God 15
  Gary W. Moon

Part I. Husband, Father and Friend 33
  The Funeral Service at Dallas's Home Church

1. If Death My Friend and Me Divide 37
  Richard J. Foster

2. Family Voices 49

  The Birth of the Books He Never Planned
  to Write—*Jane Willard*

  Living with the Great Thinker—and Feeler—*Becky Heatley*

  Give 'em Heaven—*Larissa Heatley*

  The Joy of Working with His Hands—*John Willard*

3. A Word from a Different Reality 63
  Jan Johnson

4. The Beauty of a Virtuous Man 71
  Keith Matthews

Part II. Philosopher and Professor 83
  The USC Service

5. The Evidential Force of Dallas Willard 87
  Steve L. Porter

6. Moving Beyond the Corner of the Checkerboard   98
    Greg Jesson

7. From Secular Philosophy to Faith   109
    Brandon Paradise

**8. Reflections on a Day with
My Professor and Friend**   119
    J. P. Moreland

9. Five Tips for a Teacher   130
    Gary Black Jr.

10. Widening Spheres of Influence   142

    Doing Business in the Kingdom—*Eff Martin*

    Creating in the Kingdom—*Quinton Peeples*

    Forming Education in the Kingdom—*Gayle Beebe*

    Public Service in the Kingdom—*John Kasich*

    Doing Church in the Kingdom—*John Ortberg*

**PART III. MENTOR AND
REFORMER OF THE CHURCH.**   161
The Memorial Service

**11. Master of Metanoia, Bermuda Shorts
and Wingtips**   165
    James Bryan Smith

        Sidebar: He Made Me Feel Welcome and
        Told Me a Joke—*Emilie Griffin*

12. Journey into Joy   176
    Trevor Hudson

13. Dallas Willard, Evangelist.   185
    Todd Hunter

        Sidebar: Reclaiming the
        Word *Discipleship*—*Bill Hull*

14. Developing Pastors and Churches of the Kingdom 199
   Alan Fadling

15. *Gray's Anatomy* and The Soul 203
   Mindy Caliguire

16. The Kingdom of God Is Real 208
   Kent Carlson

   Sidebar: Real Change Is Possible
   Mike Lueken

17. A Few Dallas-isms That Changed My Life 213
   Keith Meyer

18. The Real Deal 218
   Ruth Haley Barton

19. Equally at Home in Private and Public Spheres 223
   James Catford

20. Conclusion: Hey Dallas 235
   John Ortberg

Notes 243

"Lead, Kindly Light"

by John Henry Newman, 1833

Lead, kindly Light, amid th' encircling gloom, lead Thou me on!
The night is dark, and I am far from home; lead Thou me on!
Keep Thou my feet; I do not ask to see
The distant scene; one step enough for me.

I was not ever thus, nor prayed that Thou shouldst lead me on;
I loved to choose and see my path; but now lead Thou me on!
I loved the garish day, and, spite of fears,
Pride ruled my will. Remember not past years!

So long Thy power hath blest me, sure it still will lead me on.
O'er moor and fen, o'er crag and torrent, till the night is gone,
And with the morn those angel faces smile, which I
Have loved long since, and lost awhile!

Preface

Gary W. Moon

On May 4, 2013, in the earliest glow before dawn, amid the smells of disinfectant and death, the great kingdom communicator turned his face away from the friend in his room and said his last two words, apparently to the Author of his life: "Thank you."[1]

It is fitting that the last earthly words of Dallas Albert Willard would be eucharistic. He gave thanks, *eucharisteō*, echoing the words of his friend Jesus spoken before he broke a loaf of bread that made eternal living concrete for his friends. Dallas Willard spent his life making eternal living concrete for his friends. So it also seems beautifully fitting that embedded within the word *Eucharist* we find the two words that defined Dallas Willard's contagious theology: grace and joy.

Even with his last breath, it seems, he was still teaching out of lived experiences.

It is also appropriate that in the months that followed there would be not one or two but three memorial services for Dallas Willard. The kaleidoscope of memories and the diversity of the lives he had touched could not be confined to one gathering. As Aaron Preston summarized, there was a "unique grandeur" to the thinking and teaching of this man.[2]

The horizons of his knowledge were, indeed, vast and expansive. His friend and colleague Scott Soames described Dallas as "the teacher with the greatest range in the School of Philosophy at the University of Southern California."[3] But philosophy was not his only area of broad expertise. The man who chose podium over pulpit was given back both and became one of the most influential reformers of the Christian church of his generation.[4] He was also avidly read by expanding numbers of spiritual directors, Christian psychologists and a host of people in the pews who hunger for a theology that makes sense and for experiences of God that are not of this world.

It has been observed that Dallas Willard did not set out to "make a movement or foster a trend. He did *intend* to cast a big *vision* for a 'big God' in a big world."[5] Part of this "bigness" is seen in Dallas's approach to disciplines such as philosophy and biblical theology, in which, while being respectful, he was not confined by the current norms. "Instead, he focused on broad, fundamental, and enduring issues, approaching them in a way that was rigorous but nontechnical and always historically informed."[6]

The breadth of Dallas Willard's interests may best be captured by the fact that much of his writing and thought during his last decade of life rose even further above ongoing academic and ecclesiastical debates and focused on his vision for reforming the academy itself. His desire was to reclaim moral knowledge and cast a grand idea for a society where its shapers—those in the public square of business, government, entertainment, education—would practice their professions as residents of the kingdom, enrolled in "schools of life" taught by pastors and lived by all.

Given all this it was no surprise that the broad scope of Dallas Willard's interests was also reflected in the variety of individuals who attended one or more of his three memorial services. One service (May 8, 2013) was primarily for those who knew Dallas as a family member, long-time friend or adviser. The focus of another (October 4, 2013) was on those who knew Dallas best as a philosopher and colleague during his forty-seven years at USC. Between these, one tribute (May 25, 2013) gave more attention to those who knew him as a minister and reformer of the church.

The vision for creating this book is driven by Dallas Willard's influence on such a diversity of individuals. We have used the themes of the three memorials for Dallas as a way of organizing these reflections. It is not our intent to glorify or call undue attention to Dallas. Those who knew him know that he would hate that. The intent is to provide a medley of images, stories and "Dallas-isms" from many individuals who were deeply influenced by him as a family member, close friend, adviser, professor, philosopher, minister or reformer. For some who are writing, each of these labels and more may apply. The intent is for the reader to be moved and motivated toward deeper experiences of God through the sharing of stories about Dallas's influence on the lives of the writers.

Contributors have been asked to do three things. After describing special "snapshots" of time spent with Dallas, each friend explains how their shared life with Dallas has impacted their personal and professional life, and finally reflects on how these insights may be generalized to the readers of this book. Dallas Albert Willard lived a very big life. We do not present here his point of view, but a variety of points from which Dallas was viewed. We present what at times may seem like an intimate home movie—the rare kind that you actually enjoy viewing.

It should be observed that while you will be hearing from thirty voices, this chorus could have rightly included many more. Each of the thirty-one students whose dissertations Dallas chaired and the thousands of others who were students and colleagues at USC could share so much more—as could the seven hundred students who took his two-week intensive class at Fuller, the two hundred

Renovaré Institute students who devoted two years to studying his influence on Christian spiritual formation, and scores of others who knew him only through his dense and hope-filled words that became windows into the here-and-now kingdom of God.

INTRODUCTION

LIVING IN THE GLOW OF GOD

Gary W. Moon

God seems to place great value on humble beginnings. His son descended into a manger, chose rabbi school dropouts to be his students and compared the kingdom to a tiny mustard seed. There seems to be a pattern: In weakness there can be strength; in poverty, great riches.

The life of Dallas Albert Willard fits this mold. He was born on September 4, 1935, in Buffalo, Missouri, in the midst of the Great Depression. He lived his first eighteen months in a small, rented house. The small town of Buffalo was founded in 1839 as a pioneer village on the edge of the prairie and the Niangua River hills and woodlands. It was an isolated settlement that promised a fresh start for western pioneers in search of a new way to live.

Dallas was named for the county of his birth, Dallas, Missouri, which was originally organized under the name Niangua in 1841. The word *Niangua* is from an old Native American phrase meaning "I won't go away,"[1] which proved to be a poignant if not bittersweet promise to the young Dallas Willard. During the early years of his life, it seemed that people he loved very often went away.

KEEP ETERNITY BEFORE THE EYES OF THE CHILDREN

Dallas was born to Albert Alexander and Maymie Lindesmith. "Lindesmith is a German name," Dallas pointed out. "She was from Switzerland."[2] His amazing mind, unfortunately, contained no visual memories of his mother. She died in February of 1938 when he was only two and a half years old.

Maymie had jumped from a hay wagon and the impact caused a hernia. The needed surgery required a trip across the state line to a larger town, Topeka, Kansas. Dallas stayed with his maternal grandmother, Myrtle Pease, along with his three older siblings, J. I., Fran and Dwayne—who at the time were sixteen, nine and six years of age. While away, Maymie developed a fever and the surgery had to be put off for a few days. From her hospital bed she wrote poems to her children as a substitute for her loving presence.

The surgery was eventually performed, but poorly. Maymie got worse and never returned home. The last thing she said to her husband, just before she died, was, "Keep eternity before the eyes of the children."

The funeral director confirmed the family's fear that the surgeon had done a bad job. Two-year-old Dallas didn't understand what was happening, and during the funeral or wake he tried to climb into the casket to be with his mother.

Dallas was left to be raised by his father, whom he described as a "nondescript farmer, who later dabbled in local politics."[3] Dallas remembered that following the death of his mother, his father became a "crushed man," feeling somehow responsible for her death.

EARLY EDUCATION

Much of Dallas's early education was in one-room school buildings. While the dimensions of the classroom setting stayed fairly consistent, not much else did during Dallas's early years. Over the course of his time in elementary and high school he lived in multiple towns in three different counties—Dallas, Howell and Oregon. At one time or another he lived with his father and paternal grandparents; his father and stepmother, Myrtle Green; his paternal grandparents; and his older brother J. I. and his wife, Bertha. He was with J. I. and Bertha during his second- and eighth-grade years. Bertha was very young, eighteen, when five-year-old Dallas first lived with them. She once said, "I didn't raise Dallas: Dallas and I raised each other."

With all the moves and instability of these early years there were some constants: a love for learning, a love for God and the recognition of Dallas's natural gifts.

"In preschool I learned to love words; it was almost magical. I remember having appreciation for my first-grade teacher; I don't remember her name. But that first year, I discovered you could learn things, and that had been a great mystery. The discovery of learning was really huge. It opened up things. It said there are all these things and places you don't know, but you can go into them in your mind."

As might be expected, he spent much of his youth reading. He would latch on to one author and read novel after novel. Jack London was a particular favorite. "*The Sea-Wolf* was a big book for me. It is basically philosophical stuff, life work."

Dallas was baptized when he was nine years old. The pastor "was a gentle man that presented Christ in a very loving way. I had decided to go forward [to make a commitment to Christ, but] because the pastor was not there I did not go that night. I really suffered for the next week; I felt burdened. I wanted to do this thing. So the next Sunday he was there and I went forward, and it was a remarkable experience. I remember how different the world looked as I walked home in the dark. The stars, the streetlights were so different and I still have the impression that the world was really different. I felt at home in this new world. It felt like this is a good place to be; Christ is real."

Dallas was very popular in school and was elected class president his freshmen and senior years at Thomasville High School. He took that job quite seriously and was active in class reunions for decades to come. He played basketball all four years of high school and was "first string" his senior year. He also had a musical and theatrical side. Dallas graduated from Thomasville High School in 1951, as part of a graduating class of eleven people.

For most of his high school years, Dallas lived on a farm with lots of animals. He would shear sheep and help in the birthing of lambs, calves and colts. "It is hard not to love lambs," he said, "especially while watching them bounce down a hill on all fours."

MIGRANT WORKER

After graduation Dallas spent the next year and a half working as a migrant agricultural worker by day and a self-taught student by night—reading Plato and Kipling after the sun had gone down. Most of this time was spent in Oklahoma and Nebraska, but he also worked for a while in Idaho. During that time away from home Dallas also became a roofer.

Then Dallas came back to Missouri for a while and spent time with his brother J. I., who was running a large dairy farm in Liberty, near Kansas City. "He told me I had to go to college and recommended William Jewell—which was nearby—and physically took me there. After I spent some time at William Jewell, he said I had to go to Tennessee Temple. I think he knew about Tennessee Temple because he had been a reader of the periodical *Sword of the Lord*."

SPIRITUAL AWAKENING

Beginning in the fall of 1954 Dallas spent thirty months of his life in the beautiful river town of Chattanooga, Tennessee, attending Tennessee Temple College. Some might consider this an unusual starting point for someone who would later serve as director of the philosophy department at a major secular university. And at that time, the college was an unaccredited Bible school that served independent Baptist congregations—and churches that were even more conservative. But it was at this institution that Dallas had many experiences that would change the course of his life and career.

Most important, Dallas Willard met Jane Lakes of Macon, Georgia, in the library at Tennessee Temple. In Dallas's words: "Jane was this beautiful young woman. She was a student who worked in the library. She appeared so far beyond me that for a while I couldn't get the nerve to talk to her." But eventually he did.

One of the first things Jane noticed about Dallas was that he was not wearing socks. She thought he must have had a rebellious streak, a budding James Dean perhaps. She later found out he was just too poor to buy socks. They both agreed that Dallas began to frequent the library quite a lot.

It wasn't long before Dallas and Jane were participating in student-led evangelistic activities. "She would play the organ and I would sing and preach. And we would also go to surrounding, mostly black, neighborhoods with the 'good news' club. We also went to local jails and held street meetings." Dallas was listening to a radio preacher named J. Harold Smith at the time and Jane believes Dallas patterned his preaching after Smith early in his ministry.

Jane was a little older and two years ahead of Dallas in school. This helped motivate him to finish his degree in two and a half years. Jane graduated a year before Dallas, and they married before he graduated.

Academically, Dallas decided to major in psychology, in large part due to his appreciation for a professor named John Herman. "Dr. Herman was supposedly a psychologist, but he was [certainly] a teacher par excellence. He was very smart and enthusiastic. He was like Tony Campolo. High energy. He also brought a marvelous supplementation to the dead, dry Baptist orthodoxy. He was the main reason I majored in psychology."

One evening, following a special service on campus, Dallas had an unexpected encounter with God. The last thing he remembered was R. R. Brown's hand coming toward him. What followed was a vivid experience with the presence of God. "It stayed with me for days, weeks. It never left me really," Dallas said. "After that I never had the feeling that God was distant or had a problem hearing me." That night when they went to bed, Jane related, Dallas exclaimed, "There is an angel at each corner of the bed." Dallas added, "I did not have an image but a sense that they were there."

During those years Dallas stumbled across a copy of *The Imitation of Christ*—"I still have that book." He also was given a copy of *Deeper Experiences of Famous Christians*. "My friend Dudley gave me the copy. It is not a good book [from a literary perspective], but it gave me a broader view of what it meant to be a follower of Christ. It blew me out of Baptist-ism. It wasn't long until I would wear a bolo tie and a see-through shirt with the tail out, and no socks with shoes. It was getting over legalism."

ACADEMIC AWAKENING

In the fall of 1956, after graduating from Tennessee Temple, Dallas and Jane moved from Chattanooga back (for Dallas) to Thomasville, Missouri. They both taught for a few months (from September to January) in the high school Dallas had attended.

On February 16, 1957, Jane gave birth to their son, John Willard. Following John's birth, they moved from Thomasville to Waco, Texas. The move was very difficult as they were pulling the house trailer in which they would live. Along the way they endured eight flat tires, and they arrived at Baylor University with thirty-five cents in Dallas's pocket—a quarter and a dime—and a two-week-old baby in Jane's arms.

Not long after beginning studies at Baylor University—for the purpose of obtaining a second (and accredited) undergraduate degree—Dallas discovered an entirely new area of his brain: the scholarly, intellectual side. He had not thought much about a career path, by default assuming he would be a minister. But at Baylor, he recalled, "My awareness of what the life of intelligence was about deepened. I was raised so that you didn't think about things like philosophy. You figured you were just lucky to stay alive." The more Dallas thought, the more thoughtful he became. While he never lost his deep love for Scripture—that would forever keep him grounded—a new dimension was being added.

Dallas completed an undergraduate degree in religion at Baylor, but most of the coursework was in philosophy. During those two and a half years in Waco he also completed all the units necessary for a master's in psychology, but did not claim the degree. It didn't matter. The degree was secondary to something much more important. It was while he was in the graduate program that he began to hear discussions about the kingdom of God.

After Dallas completed his work at Baylor, he moved with Jane and John to Warner Robbins, Georgia, near Jane's hometown of Macon. Jane taught junior high school and Dallas taught high school in Warner Robbins. Dallas also served as associate pastor at Avandel Baptist Church in Macon, where Jane had attended as a child.

It was during that year, Dallas reported, that he became convicted about how little he knew about God and the soul. "I was totally incapable of making any sense of God and the human soul and decided during that winter to go back to graduate school in philosophy for a couple of years just to improve my understanding. I had no intent to take a degree."

"At the end of that summer of 1959, we loaded up a U-Haul and drove up Highway 41 all the way from Macon to downtown Chicago and then on to Madison. Little John was in the back seat; he was two years old."

Dallas began studies at the University of Wisconsin in the fall of 1959 and completed a PhD in 1964. The degree "included a major in philosophy and a minor in the history of science." He also picked up a second degree in fatherhood. Becky Willard was born on February 17, 1962, at the University Hospital, where Jane was also an employee.

During Dallas's time at the University of Wisconsin, three things happened that would change his life and, perhaps, the face of evangelicalism.

First, Dallas met and became friends with a number of individuals who helped him gain a vision for the importance of the academy to the kingdom and for the university as a place of evangelism. Stan Matson, part of the InterVarsity group on campus; John Alexander, who later became head of InterVarsity worldwide; David Noble, who would go on to start Summit Ministries; and Harold Myra, who later became president of *Christianity Today*, were all important to Dallas. However, it was Earl Aldridge, a professor in the Spanish department, who echoed words Dallas says he had already heard spoken by God into his fertile mind: "If you go to the church you will have the church, but if you go to the university the churches will also be given."

The second game-changing discovery was the subject of Dallas's dissertation: Edmund Husserl, the father of phenomenology.[4] While we will devote an entire chapter of this volume to the importance of Husserl to Dallas Willard's thinking, it is important to hear about this connection in Dallas's own words.

"Husserl offered an explanation of consciousness in all its forms that elucidates why realism is possible. He helped me to understand that in religion you also have *knowledge* and you are dealing with reality. What Jesus taught was a source of knowledge, real knowledge, and not merely an invitation to a leap of faith. . . . Husserl does not allow you to get in a position to say all you have is a story. You live in a world that is *real*, and this applies to morality as well as to physics. . . . Science took over the university and [in the process] we lost values and morality, and that is the crisis. And postmodernism is a reaction to the idea that science is the only way."

After hearing Dallas explain this I asked him, "Is this why your theology seems to me to be more at home in the church of the first few centuries than with modern evangelicalism?" His quick response: "Absolutely! The early church did not get stuck in a Cartesian box. Aristotle thought there were a real world and a real mind that could know it. And that is what disappears. I have watched scientists listen to postmodernists and it is a constant display of thinly veiled disgust."

Husserl helped Dallas defend the notion that Jesus was describing a *knowable* reality when he talked about the kingdom and the Trinity. But there was an additional result from Dallas's time in Madison. He began to believe in his ability to "do philosophy" in a high-level academic setting.

The third thing was acceptance by the academic community. Dallas described what happened after he presented a paper: "The paper I presented was a turning point because I wrote that and read it to a philosophy group and they were impressed. After that my peers and the faculty treated me differently." Dallas's eyes may have reflected just a hint of pride. "It called my attention to, 'Okay, Willard, you can do this type of philosophy,' and that was very important to the future. It went along with passing the final exams. Most of that paper was incorporated into my dissertation (first chapter) and the basic point has been substantial to everything I've done: you don't get a special clarity by talking about language."

Dallas completed his PhD at the University of Wisconsin in 1964 and taught there for one year. In the fall of 1965, when Dallas was thirty years old, he and Jane, John and Becky moved from Madison, Wisconsin, to Los Angeles, California, where he had accepted a position in the philosophy department at the University of Southern California. They traveled along historic Route 66 for much of the trip.

We are now entering the time in Dallas's life when, through his role as professor and mentor to ministers, he began to meet many individuals who have authored these chapters. I will provide just a few more highlights before tagging out to the other voices.

PROFESSOR AND MINISTER TO MINISTERS

Dallas Willard was greatly admired as a professor and contributor to student life at USC. In 1976 he won the Blue Key National Honor Fraternity "Outstanding Faculty Member" award for his contributions to student life. In 1977 he received the USC Associates Award for Excellence in Teaching. In 1984 he won the USC Student Senate Award for Outstanding Faculty of the Year, and in 2000 he was named the Gamma Sigma Delta Professor of the Year. Indeed, for three years (fall of 1981 through spring of 1984) the Willards lived *with* the students while participating in USC's Faculty in Residence program.

From 1982 to 1985 Dallas served as the director of the School of Philosophy. But in his words, "I became department chair only because some leading members of the faculty came to me and said you must do this. I only did this so they would not ask me to do it again. I had it firmly in my mind that I did not come there to administer."

While Dallas was pouring his life into the lives of students and faculty members at USC, he also began to have significant "accidental" mentoring relationships with ministers who would in time have a great impact on the church.[5] One of these key relationships may never have happened except for Dallas and Jane's decision to move out into the country.

After spending their first year on the West Coast in Mar Vista in West Hollywood, Dallas and Jane bought a house in Chatsworth, California, and lived there together for almost forty-six years—excluding the three years they lived on the USC campus. The house is small and sits on top of the ridge of a small mountain. The terrain is very rocky and the surrounding area so remote that it was used for the making of many Western films and television series. It could be argued that if the rock population were diminished a bit and the ground more flat, Dallas had found the closest thing to rural Missouri that existed within an hour's drive of the USC campus. When four-year-old Becky Willard found a frog in a gopher hole, the real estate deal was done.

Not long after moving to Chatsworth, the Willards began attending a small Friends church on Woodlake Avenue in the fall of 1966. "We went because of the pastor, Jim Hewitt. He preached good sermons, had a master's in English literature and was a Fuller graduate. Jim became really involved in our lives. He left to become a Presbyterian."

In the fall of 1969 the Friends denomination sent a young, fresh out of seminary student to pastor the Woodlake Avenue Church. His name was Richard J. Foster. Dallas said, "I thought, *Now here is a lovely, smart young man. He is a winning man.* And basically we started talking and never stopped."

I'll leave it to Richard himself to tell the rest of that story (see chapter two). But to say the least, the two men formed a beautiful friendship, which eventually led to the creation of the ministry Renovaré and ignited a movement that some would argue has become one of the most significant happenings in the church during the past century.

Richard J. Foster represents a multitude in the church world who were drawn to the ideas of the professional philosopher, amateur theologian and practical mystic Dallas Willard. And I think each would say that more inviting than his fresh ideas was the fact that Dallas lived what he believed. As John Ortberg put it, "he lived in another time zone."[6]

THE REALLY BIG IDEAS

There have been several attempts to capture Dallas Willard's big ideas. In 2007 the Renovaré Institute was established to provide a two-year study experience that allows students to systematically soak in the twelve critical concepts of Renovaré—the majority of which can be traced directly or indirectly to the thinking of Dallas Willard.[7] The most concise presentation of Dallas's vision for Christian spiritual formation and churches becoming "schools of life" is found in his own words, in brief summaries of his primary Christian writings. He described his books this way:

> In the first, *In Search of Guidance*, I attempted to make real and clear the intimate quality of life with [Jesus] as "a conversational relationship with God."
>
> But that relationship is not something that automatically happens, and we do not receive it by passive infusion. So the second book, *The Spirit of the Disciplines*, explains how disciples or students of Jesus can effectively interact with the grace and spirit of God to access fully the provisions and character intended for us in the gift of eternal life.
>
> However, actual discipleship or apprenticeship to Jesus is, in our day, no longer thought of as in any way essential to faith in him. . . . The third book, then, presents discipleship to Jesus as the very heart of the gospel. The really good news for humanity is that Jesus is now taking students in the master class of life. The eternal life that begins with confidence in Jesus is a life in his present kingdom, now on earth and available to all.[8]

It could be argued that the key purpose for *Renovation of the Heart* was to provide understanding concerning how to bring the various dimensions of the human self under God's reign, and *Knowing Christ Today* sought to underscore that knowledge of the reality of Christ is available through interactive experience of the Trinity.

I believe that if one were asked to identify a single golden thread that runs through each of Dallas Willard's books—a key idea that sets his thinking apart from so many others—it would be the idea that it is actually possible to step into the words of John 17:3 and enter into an experiential relationship, a transforming friendship, with the Trinity. In the words of Steve Porter, an ordinary person can grab hold of life from above.[9] An ordinary person can live a "with-God" life—surrendered and obedient to divine will.

PAIN, PRESENCE, LIGHT, KNOWLEDGE AND SCRIPTURE

Sometimes in intimate conversation, Dallas's face would show lines of regret and his eyes would drop when he confessed wishing he had been a better husband and father. But it was in that pain that he found a powerful God—residing at, as he might say, "the-end-of-my-rope.com." Dallas did not start breathing the Lord's Prayer and twenty-third Psalm before getting out of bed for the purpose of keeping a devotional score card. Instead, he had entered a time of suffering so intense that he did not want to put his feet on the floor before being reassured that his Father's kingdom is a good and perfectly safe place.

Dallas shared the memory that as a boy he would try to cut wood for neighbors just right, a perfect fit for the fireplace or wood stove, because, he reasoned, if you please people you may be asked to stay for a while. It may well be that the pain caused by the sudden absence of a loved one created a deep desire for presence in Dallas's life that eventually led him to the greatest discovery and most important theme of his writing: We can live our lives in a constant and transforming friendship with a loving God, who will never go away, and who is not that picky about how wood is cut.

In addition to Dallas's belief in the here, now and forever presence and experiential reality of God, he also seemed fascinated by the light, energy and glow of God. It could be said that he was an unlikely and ultra-practical mystic. But understand, by using the term *mystic* I simply mean that he believed God is present in a real sense and that when you talk with him a two-way conversation is possible. And for Dallas, the light and life of God was very real and present.

Two of the churches he attended for long periods of time were a Quaker and a Vineyard congregation. It could be argued that geography and Jane's appreciation for the Vineyard were the key factors for those church choices. But Dallas was particularly drawn to the life and ministry of John Wimber, and was deeply appreciative of the healing ministries of Bill Vaswig and Agnes Sanford and her book *The Healing Light*. Environments where the experience of God could be celebrated and expected seemed to have a magnetic attraction for Dallas.

While Dallas Willard may have been a practical mystic, a person for whom the presence and light of God were as real as the flow of electricity into a light bulb, there were two factors that contributed mightily to the profoundness of his thinking and writing about these themes. The first is his connection to Edmund Husserl; the second is his connection to Scripture.

Dallas believed people will indeed perish for lack of *knowledge*, but may find eternal living through *knowledge* of the Trinity. In fact, because of the impact of Husserl on his thinking, Dallas actually believed that while much of the modern world and most in the academy have lost knowledge as the center of what matters most, knowledge of God is not only possible but also ultimately as measurable as events in a physics laboratory. His evangelistic efforts were not to produce a leap of faith but interactive knowledge of God.

Pain. Presence. Light. Knowledge. And Scripture. Dallas Willard's life experiences provided this Southern Baptist minister, professional philosopher, amateur theologian and practical mystic with an appreciation for and approach to Scripture that was most unusual. He was able to simultaneously maintain a high view and deep love of the Bible—as evidenced by the wear on the cover and the notes scribbled in most every margin—while being able to view it in a way that was outside most Christian boxes.

He was able to approach Scripture with the reverence of a Southern Baptist, the mind of a respected philosopher and the vision of a mystic. The result appears to be a theology and view of God that is much more at home in the early church than with modern evangelicalism. And that's the whole deal. Dallas Willard was a reformer of the modern evangelical church, pointing back to its early roots and across the centuries to times when lives were being transformed through participation in the here, now and real life with the Trinity.

MEETING DALLAS

My first encounter with Dallas Willard was in the late fall of 1989 and was very dramatic—even though he was more than 2,400 miles away. It was one of those few moments in life that becomes seared into memory and never forgotten. I still remember the pattern of color on the sofa where I lay reading, the rough texture of the blue book in my hand, my musing whether I'd save ink by underlining what was unimportant, and the picture on the wall that my eyes landed on after I looked up from the words on the page and thought, "This is what I've been waiting to read my entire life." Dallas's words gave me hope that the gap between the high-sounding promises of Jesus and the low-lying practices of my Christian walk could be closed.

The book was *The Spirit of the Disciplines.* It was recommended to me by a friend as a must-read. I followed his advice because I enjoyed reading *Celebration of Discipline* nine years earlier as part of a class Richard J. Foster was teaching at Fuller Seminary in 1980.

Within a few months I asked both Dallas Willard and Richard Foster to be part of an advisory board for something I was putting together called The Institute of Clinical Theology. To my great surprise each said yes, and each later agreed to be a speaker at two separate conferences to be held by the institute.

Dallas spoke at the first of the conferences. It was held in Virginia Beach in the spring of 1992. Before the event Dallas sat in our small house—I did not realize he would have considered it a big house—

eating coconut cake on the sofa where I had first been exposed to his thinking. He was fifty-six years old.

We drove to the event and he started the conference with a line that warmed my heart: "All theology should be clinical theology." The only fan letter I ever wrote I put in his hands as he was leaving for the airport.

For the next two decades I tried to find some reason, some excuse to stay connected to this warm, gentle and brilliant man. He was the principal speaker at a 1995 Christian Association for Psychological Studies (CAPS) conference on soul care. (Thomas Oden also spoke and proclaimed it to be the first conference held under the banner of soul care in psychology or pastoral care.) That is when I found out that Jane Willard was an innovative psychotherapist who had been pioneering work in guided imagery involving Jesus in inner healing prayer—and that both Dallas and Jane had a great sense of humor.

It wasn't long—1999 to be specific—before Dallas agreed to lend his name to *Conversations* journal. This was only fair since it was his articulation of the components of the person that formed the departments or section of the publication, and it was his and Richard Foster's emphasis on the great Christian traditions that motivated the publication to be balanced and ecumenical.

Then came his participation in a small group curriculum series inspired by some of his and Richard Foster's books and put together under the label "Curriculum of Christlikeness." I never asked him why he continued to say there was no curriculum of Christlikeness. But I do remember hearing his deep baritone voice for the first time when after a long technical delay during a filming session he led the group in singing, "This is my story, this is my song, praising my Savior all the day long." We worked on these projects from early 2000 to 2013.

I just kept asking and he kept saying yes—to interviews, speaking events and conversations. But by far the yes that led to the most intense and inspiring times was when he agreed to teach in the Renovaré Institute. Over the course of five years (2007 to 2013), there were wonderful times of preparation and six weeks of intensive teaching to three different groups of over forty students in Menlo Park, Denver and Atlanta. Dallas would not only teach for three sessions a day but would also insist on meeting with each student who wanted to meet with him one on one. Less than two months before his death he addressed the fourth cohort group in Santa Barbara. It was his last public teaching. He was a shadow of himself and taught from a chair. I said my second-to-last goodbye to him from a bench at La Casa de Maria. I have never witnessed such a powerful example of love for others, and I don't expect I ever will again.

My decision in 2011 to serve as the director of the Dallas Willard Center at Westmont College was one of the easiest decisions of my life. And it made the unexpected death of Dallas Willard in 2013 one of the most painful experiences of my life. The man who had lived with eternity before his eyes also followed the advice he gave from his deathbed to his granddaughter, Larissa. He kept giving away heaven and reminding us that it is a place that surrounds us all, as close as the air we breathe, as close as our heavenly Father.

PART ONE

Husband, Father and Friend

The Funeral Service
at Dallas's Home Church

On May 8, 2013, the funeral for Dallas Albert Willard was conducted before a small gathering of approximately 150 individuals, most of whom had known him intimately as a family member, relative or long-time friend. The service was held in a converted commercial building that still looked at home in the surrounding neighborhood of apartments and small businesses.[1] The one-story structure was across the street from a vacant lot and nestled between a pharmacy and a parking lot for boats. Dallas and Jane Willard had been making the twenty-minute drive to attend services in the small church for more than two decades.

Entering the facility was somewhat like stepping into the Tardis—it seemed bigger on the inside.[2] The sanctuary was a large, windowless room with a lowered ceiling. A simple wooden cross and a couple of cloth banners were the only religious imagery in a space that could be reset to host a civic gathering in a matter of minutes.

The first speaker, Lynn Cory, associate pastor at Valley Vineyard, stepped behind a wooden podium and read two verses that he suggested framed Dallas Willard's life: "Take My yoke upon you and learn from Me, for I am gentle and lowly in heart, and you will find rest for your souls. For My yoke is easy and My burden is light" (Mt 11:29-30 NKJV).

Two songs chosen by Dallas Willard followed the introduction. The first, "Shall We Gather at the River?," was to be sung, as Dallas had instructed in a handwritten note to his daughter, Becky, "not like a dirge, but triumphant."

Soon we'll reach the shining river,
soon our pilgrimage will cease;
soon our happy hearts will quiver
with the melody of peace.

The haunting words from the final verse were still causing tears to slide down cheeks when the second song began, "In Christ Alone."

Most of the individuals who spoke that day have written essays for this volume. Each was either a family member or member of Dallas Willard's ministry advisory committee. Bill Dwyer (Dallas's pastor at Valley Vineyard Christian Fellowship), Keith Matthews, Jan Johnson, Larissa Heatley and Jane Willard offered a medley of memories of how their dear friend, grandfather and husband had interlaced their lives in ways that warmed their hearts. For them, Dallas's often-repeated blessing over food was fulfilled. He was the kind of person who caused you to be glad God made the world and put him in it.[3]

These warm eulogies were followed by a haunting video of a magical conversation between John Ortberg and Dallas that had happened less than three months prior, at Dallas's second-to-last public appearance.[4] Quite prophetically, Dallas spoke the following words at his own funeral:

"Your moment of passage from this earth will be one of great joy. . . . We begin to live in heaven now. That is why those who begin to keep his word will not experience death. [You will] continue to exist as the people you are in the presence of God. Many people will not realize they died until later, and they will recognize that something is different."

Then Dallas, with tears in his eyes, began to quote the first line from one of his favorite hymns, "Lead, Kindly Light."

> Lead, kindly Light, amid th' encircling gloom,
> lead Thou me on!
> The night is dark, and I am far from home;
> lead Thou me on!
> Keep Thou my feet; I do not ask to see
> The distant scene; one step enough for me.

The video faded from the screen, and Steve Emerson sang "Finally Home."

> But just think of stepping on shore—And finding it heaven!
> Of touching a hand—And finding it God's!
> Of breathing new air—And finding it celestial!
> Of waking up in glory—And finding it home!

The body of Dallas Willard was wheeled in a few minutes before the funeral service. A few of those present walked by to see their friend one last time. The battle with cancer had taken its toll. The former "house" of Dallas was a dim shadow of its former glory, and it silently proclaimed that its unceasing spiritual tenant existed at a new address.

1

IF DEATH MY FRIEND
AND ME DIVIDE

Richard J. Foster

The message on the answering machine is brief, almost cryptic. It is the tone in the voice that catches my attention: bone weary and sad beyond telling. "The situation is more grave than I allowed Becky to share in the email to everyone. From a human perspective there is no hope. I wanted you to know."

The voice is that of Jane Willard. The "situation" is the stage four cancer Dallas is battling and specifically the latest exploratory surgery to discover the reason he is not able to consume food. With my heart racing I quickly dial Jane's private number, and wonderfully she picks up. Briefly, Jane fills me in on the doctor's report from the surgery. The news is devastating! The chemo and radiation treatments of the past months have not succeeded. The cancer has grown aggressively and now blocks the intestinal tract. The doctors explain that they have done everything within their powers and have now run out of options.

We share quietly, confidentially. We agree that I will come for a final, private visit—spending the morning with Dallas (as much as his energy will allow), lunch with Bill and Becky, and the afternoon with Jane. Providentially, I have just enough time between speaking engagements to make the trip. Hurriedly I gather a few things into a travel bag and call the airline. My mind drifts back to those early days together in 1970.

(((

Fresh out of six years of graduate work, I was assigned by my denomination to a small church plant in southern California. On the surface Woodlake Avenue Friends Church looked like a ragtag group, a kind of marginal failure on the ecclesiastical scoreboards. Looking a little deeper, though, I quickly discovered an astonishing kaleidoscope of human personalities—and prominent among them were Dallas and Jane Willard and their children, John and Becky.

Even before I met Dallas, I knew of his reputation as a world-class philosopher. However, in our small fellowship Dallas was simply the person who led the singing (what we today would call the worship leader), while Jane played the organ (remember those days?).

Early on I was struck by the love and care that Dallas shared with Tony, another member of our fellowship. Tony was a construction worker with little formal education. Tony could not possibly have understood Dallas's work in philosophy, but no matter. A bond of love and fellowship in Christ existed between these two that was quite wonderful to watch. They would gather at Dallas's home once a week, just the two of them, to study the Bible and pray together.

In the early weeks of my coming to Woodlake there was an emergency that put Jane in the hospital. Tony called me to say, "We need to call the church together to pray for Jane and Dallas." And so we did. For three nights straight. How moving to observe Tony, in his earnest, Italian-laden accent, imploring God for healing and for an all-encompassing sense of divine Presence to surround Jane and Dallas. Some time later I learned that Tony, who worked all day on a heavy construction crew, had been fasting throughout those three days on behalf of Jane and Dallas. What a vivid example of Christian koinonia!

(((

The drive to the Denver airport is a blur. I am on autopilot. I don't even remember turning onto the freeway. Arriving at the airport early I check in and make my way through the security lines. My normal pattern upon arriving early would be a little exercise routine of walking the concourse back and forth until my flight is ready. Not today. Finding my way to the departure gate I slip into a seat and wait in complete silence. Crowds are rushing here and there, but I am totally insulated within my own thoughts.

(((

The friendship that Dallas and I experienced in those early years of ministry together grew rapidly. I would do the preaching but Dallas and I would trade off teaching assignments at the church. Years later I would explain that when I taught people might come, but when Dallas taught they brought their tape recorders. Me too. I probably have a hundred old, scratchy audiotapes of Dallas teaching us.

One of the early courses was an astonishing series in the book of Acts. It was there that one of Dallas's most famous sentences was born: "The aim of God in history is the creation of an all-inclusive community of loving persons with God himself at the very center of this community as its prime Sustainer and most glorious Inhabitant." Dallas took us on a whirlwind tour of human history, showing how God had revealed this aim for an all-inclusive community of loving persons to all the great religious faiths; from the Upanishads in India to Gautama the Buddha and Mahavira, from Confucius and Lao-Tzu in China to Zarathustra in Persia, to the preexilic prophets in Israel. During those centuries of God's revelation it became clear that sacrifices, ceremonies, propitiations and other externalities ceased to be sufficient to make up the religious life, and the principle of peace on earth to all persons of good will swept across the face of the earth.

The special vocation of the Jewish people in God's plan was to embody this Divine-human community by dwelling in God and by bringing all nations in. The Jewish nation failed in this by becoming simply another, though still very special, humanly based social unit. However, the Jewish nation, in spite of itself, ultimately succeeded in fulfilling God's purposes by preparing an adequate social basis for the reception of this Divine-human community, the kingdom of God.

"In the fullness of time" Jesus Christ, the God-man, came, fulfilling the prophetic messianic vision. Following Jesus' life, death and resurrection this aim of God for the creation of an all-inclusive community could become embodied in the incendiary fellowship of Christ followers.

The book of Acts now came alive as we studied it through the lens of this aim of God for the formation of an all-inclusive community of loving persons without any cultural presuppositions whatsoever. We came to understand the many obstacles to the formation of such a community and how the Holy Spirit led these followers of "the Way," step by step, to overcome these obstacles. Most particularly we watched as the early disciples of Jesus worked their way through the crucial issue of the Jewish cultural captivity of the church, reaching its dramatic climax at the Jerusalem Council in Acts 15. Then too we came to see the significance of Paul's warnings against a future Gentile cultural captivity of the church—which indeed did occur in the centuries to follow and which we struggle with to this very day.

(((

I am startled by the gate agent announcing the standard boarding instructions. Passengers rise and begin boarding. I linger back a bit, not relishing the thought of being crammed together with this mass of humanity. As is common these days the flight is filled to capacity. Making my way into the plane I am thankful to be assigned an aisle seat; somehow it gives me a measure of private space. One thing I do appreciate about airplanes is the anonymity they afford. No one knows me. No one asks about anything. Today, I am glad to be anonymous. I ease back into the seat and close my eyes . . .

(((

I will always cherish the course Dallas taught our little fellowship on the Sermon on the Mount. As a teenager I had read Dietrich Bonhoeffer's The Cost of Discipleship *over and over, so taken was I by Bonhoeffer's analysis of the Sermon on the Mount. So when Dallas immersed us in this most important of Jesus' teachings on virtue ethics, I was utterly captivated. Throughout my seminary training I had given special attention to the Sermon on the Mount. I knew the literature in the field; I knew the varying approaches and interpretations of the text. Hence, I recognized immediately that what Dallas was teaching us was stunningly creative and life giving, and at the same time deeply rooted in classical thought. Of course, whenever Dallas taught one section of the Bible he ended up roaming across the entire biblical canon. It was astonishing! The content of those teaching sessions is essentially what we have today in* The Divine Conspiracy.

Our little group hung on every word. "We are on to something big," I thought to myself, "something really big." Such teachings completely transformed our fellowship, especially in terms of genuine character formation. Friends and neighbors saw these changes in our people, and our fellowship grew.

(((

The plane skidding on the runway jars me into the present moment. While I want to continue in the memories of forty years of friendship and ministry, I do need to deal with the realities at hand: picking up my bag, securing the rental car, driving to the motel, checking in, eating, sleeping.

Early the next morning, with coffee in hand, I make my way to a nice inner courtyard with lush plants and a fountain to help muffle the motel sounds. I sit there for some time quietly sipping my coffee.

(((

Sometimes Dallas could help us as an entire congregation with a simple comment of accumulated wisdom. One Sunday morning I was preaching on Moses and how he needed to learn to do the work of the Lord in the power of the Spirit. Moses, of course, had tried to do God's work in the flesh by killing the Egyptian, and it had failed miserably. So God had to put him into the desert for forty years to learn to do the work of God in the power of the Spirit.

In the context of our Quaker worship practice, it is perfectly appropriate for any person in the fellowship to speak a timely word from the Lord. As I was beginning to wax eloquent, in my enthusiasm I said something like, "Now, we want to learn these lessons so that it won't take us forty years like it did Moses." Dallas, in his great wisdom, simply spoke up so everyone could hear, "I doubt it."

Of course his comment stopped my sermon right in mid-sentence— and it needed to be stopped! His remark forced us to consider the hidden preparation through which God puts his ministers. It deeply influenced the manner in which we did ministry from that day forward. We were learning the delicate balance of not running ahead of the Spirit, nor of lagging behind. We were learning the cosmic patience of God and how we were to come into the rhythms of the Holy Spirit.

(((

The chiming of my cell phone interrupts my thoughts. It is Jane. "I'm wondering if you could come a little earlier than we scheduled. We may need to take Dallas to the hospital for hydration. He can't seem to get any liquids down." Quickly I jump up and drive the few miles to the Willard address and up the steep, narrow driveway I remember so well. Jane comes out to greet me and we hug tightly, sorrowfully. I slip into the study while Jane goes to get Dallas. I glance around the study. It looks exactly the same as it has all these forty-plus years of our friendship: the couch, the grand piano where Jane sometimes plays, the chair by the fireplace, the books scattered about, and in the adjoining room, Dallas's desk with many more books. How well I remember this place.

(((

In those intensive days of ministering together I would often come to Dallas's home study and we would sit together, discussing and praying for the people in our fellowship. The grace and love and care that he carried for each person was always moving to me as pastor. Then, often we would slip into complete silence—a listening silence of course. Sometimes the phone would ring or perhaps someone would knock at the door, but Dallas would never flinch. He was present to the Lord and present to me. I will always cherish those times of silence, for we had not only come together, but we were gathered together in the power of the Lord.

(((

Dallas comes in, weak but with a warm smile. Jane eases him into the big chair by the fireplace. I have come from Denver to Chatsworth to say goodbye to an old friend. Dallas has come from bedroom to study for the same reason. His journey is the harder.

We share about trivialities, like old friends do. I mention that last night I drove by the shiny hospital complex where Woodlake Avenue Friends Church had once stood. "The church is gone," I say, "and the Ramsey nursery as well." Ever the philosopher, Dallas pauses briefly and then replies, "They aren't really gone, you know; they are held in the mind of God. A day will come when you can visit them again . . . if you want to."

Knowing Dallas's great love of the Wesley brothers, I share with him the poetic words of Charles Wesley:

If death my friend and me divide,
thou dost not, Lord, my sorrow chide,
or frown my tears to see;
restrained from passionate excess,
thou bidst me mourn in calm distress
for them that rest in thee.

I feel a strong immortal hope,
which bears my mournful spirit up
beneath its mountain load;
redeemed from death, and grief, and pain,
I soon shall find my friend again
within the arms of God.

Pass a few fleeting moments more
and death the blessing shall restore
which death has snatched away;
for me thou wilt the summons send,
and give me back my parted friend
in that eternal day.

We sit together in absolute silence. Then with trembling voice I say, "Dallas, we may not see each other again . . ." Our conversation is interrupted as Bill and Becky arrive and we need to take Dallas to the hospital. There the customary flurry of doctors and nurses and medical staff goes on and on. All day long.

There is one brief period when Dallas and Jane and Bill and Becky and I are together without medical staff. I suggest we pray and everyone readily agrees. Articulating the prayer is left to me. How do you pray for a friend who is nearing the valley of the shadow? I want to pray for his healing, but I need to prepare for his dying. There is no contradiction in this. It is a simple recognition that *we* are not in charge of the issues of life and death. I begin my prayer by lifting Dallas into the healing life and light of Jesus Christ, inviting Jesus to do what is right and good for him. Dallas seems to take in the prayer with tender sighs.

Back at the house Dallas is helped into an easy chair near the TV. John, Dallas and Jane's son, is there, and it is so good to catch up with his story for we have not seen each other for some time. Graciously Larissa, Bill and Becky's daughter, has baked a birthday cake for me; I had forgotten about my birthday. Eventually we gather in the study and eat and celebrate with birthday cake. We chatter on into the evening.

Finally it is time for me to leave. I go in to say goodbye to my old friend for the last time. Dallas takes my hand and speaks as if to continue the conversation of the morning. He smiles and says ever so tenderly and ever so firmly, "We *will* see each other again!"

I fly home. I'm glad for the solitude of the airplane.

Four days later I am boarding an early flight to Detroit. My cell rings; it is my wife Carolynn with the heartbreaking news that at 5:55 this morning Dallas stepped over from this life into greater Life. In come a flurry of calls from magazine editors wanting a statement or an essay for their webpage. Boarding the plane I turn my cell off. It is going to be a long flight. I sit isolated and alone in this missile of steel as it is being hurtled across the country.

)))

It seems like only yesterday that Carolynn and I were traveling with Dallas and Jane in Florence, Italy. Now, to explore the streets of Florence with Dallas is like traveling with a walking encyclopedia. Just because Dallas knew of my keen interest in the medieval preacher Girolamo Savonarola, he took me to the piazza where Savonarola had been executed and pointed out the plaque smack in the middle of the cobblestone street that marked the spot of his hanging.

Then as we toured one of the many art galleries in Florence, Dallas had some special insight or pearl of wisdom about every painting. Every single painting! I was reduced to saying things like, "Oh, yeah,

sure, I knew that!" Finally I confessed, "You know, Dallas, I guess
there is this huge gap in my education in Renaissance art." He smiled
and said simply, "Oh, that's all right. You will have all of eternity to
fill in the gap."

"All of eternity . . ." At conferences Dallas would often teach that
we are "unceasing spiritual beings with an eternal destiny in God's
great universe." Well, my friend Dallas Albert Willard has now
stepped more fully than ever before into this "eternal destiny in God's
great universe."

〈〈〈

My flight lands in Detroit, and for the next several days I will be
engaged in a variety of teaching sessions. When I travel my pattern
is to be as fully present as possible to the people and activities of
the moment. So, when traveling there is no multitasking for me. No
cell phone calls. No extraneous interviews. No catching up on
email. No browsing the Internet. Indeed, I don't even bring my
laptop with me. For this particular trip this practice is a great grace,
for I am spared all the Internet and social media buzz that is no
doubt going on over Dallas's death. Instead, I am able to mourn
inwardly and reflect on the significance and the legacy of the one
who has been taken from us.

For us a great light has gone out. We are diminished by Dallas's
passing. How does one assess such a person, such a life?

Dallas's published writings will endure and no doubt increase
in importance as time passes. He left many unpublished writings
(I have seen them in stacks scattered throughout his study), and
I can well imagine that others will be working with this huge
legacy so that eventually more books by Dallas will be published
than he ever published in his lifetime. His massive contribution
in his chosen field of philosophy has barely been touched, and I
expect scholars will be exploring his thinking in this arena for
some time.

Of course Dallas's brilliance, as important as it is, is far from the whole story. He possessed in his person a spiritual formation into Christlikeness that was simply astonishing to all who were around him. Profound character formation had transpired in his body and mind and spirit until love, joy, peace, patience, kindness, goodness, faithfulness, gentleness and self-control were at the very center of the deep habit-structures of his life. He exhibited a substantively transformed life. Dallas was simply soaked in the presence of the living Christ.

Now, I say these things not as someone looking admiringly from a distance. Dallas and I worked together and knew each other for more than forty years. I knew the warts and the wrinkles. Still, I saw rich character-forming realities deepen and thicken in Dallas over many years.

I am struggling for the words to share with you what I mean. To put it negatively, Dallas was amazingly free from guile and manipulation and control. To say it positively, he showed graciousness and kindness and gentleness to everyone who came in contact with him. The old word for what I am trying to get at is *holiness*. But in our day this word has been so corrupted that it cannot carry the weight of what I am after. Perhaps the phrase *unadulterated goodness* captures what I saw in Dallas as well as anything I can think of. He truly was a good man.

Such a life formation does not occur instantaneously or automatically. The practice of Christian spiritual disciplines is fundamental to such character transformation. Dallas, of course, taught us about these matters constantly: classical disciplines of abstinence such as solitude, silence, fasting, frugality, chastity, secrecy and sacrifice; classical disciplines of engagement such as study, worship, celebration, service, prayer, fellowship, confession and submission. (See *The Spirit of the Disciplines*.)

These are the disciplines Dallas engaged in throughout his life in order to train his body, mind and spirit into deep, inward habits of goodness; as Paul admonished, "Train yourself in godliness" (1 Tim

4:7 NRSV). And we are witnesses to the effects of such a life of training. Dallas was someone whose life was penetrated throughout by love, who possessed a faith that could see everything in the light of God's overriding governance for good, and who could access the supernatural power of God to overcome evil and do what is right. In our own lives and in the days that lie before us we will do well to follow his lead.

(((

When I was with Dallas four days before he died I had in my bag the book *The Last Battle*, the final volume in C. S. Lewis's Chronicles of Narnia series. I brought it along thinking we might share a passage or two together. As things turned out there was no opportunity that day. Right now one passage from this book seems to speak particularly well to the present situation. It is the last paragraph of this last book in the series. The context is the end of the children's adventures, for they have all died in a train wreck. Lewis writes,

> The things that began to happen . . . were so great and beautiful that I cannot write them. And for us this is the end of all the stories, and we can most truly say that they all lived happily ever after. But for them it was only the beginning of the real story. All their life in this world and all their adventures in Narnia had only been the cover and the title page: now at last they were beginning Chapter One of the Great Story which no one on earth has read: which goes on forever: in which every chapter is better than the one before.[1]

And so it is.

Goodbye, my friend. "We *will* see each other again!"

Richard J. Foster is the founder of Renovaré. He is the author of many books, including *Celebration of Discipline* and, most recently, *Sanctuary of the Soul*.

2

FAMILY VOICES

The Birth of the Books
He Never Planned to Write

- Jane Willard -

One day it occurred to me that Dallas did not initiate the idea of writing any of his books on Christian spirituality. In contrast, all of his work in philosophy was self-initiated. When I realized this a few years ago, I thought that fact sort of fit in with his description of his years of teaching. He once playfully explained that he never thought of himself as having a career—"it is more of a careen," he said, meaning that he just fell into it.

From the time that I met Dallas in college, where he preached in jail services and at street meetings, I saw that his preaching was a response to the call of God. Wherever we lived, whatever kind of employment he might have had, he also preached or taught the Word of God. With every invitation he received, he heard in his mind, "Woe is me if I preach not the gospel." Writing was a different issue. Dallas did not plan to write Christian books; even though I often suggested that writing is one way of preaching, this seemed never to fit in his mind.

Hearing God [first published as *In Search of Guidance*], for example, was initiated by one of Dallas's USC graduate students,

Randy Neal. I wrote Randy recently to get exact details on how the book came to be written, and Randy began with, "He did it for me, plain and simple!"

An editor at Gospel Light Publications knew Randy and called to ask if he could get Dallas to contribute to their new "In Search of" series. Randy told me that when he spoke with him, Dallas asked a few questions, then concluded, "I don't have time right now to write a book; but I do have audiotapes of a series I recently presented. If you would be willing to transcribe those cassettes into a rough text, then I'll edit the transcripts and you can have the royalty advance in order to help you along your way."

So Randy transcribed Dallas's recorded teaching sessions, and Dallas revised the material into chapters. Randy had a wife and three children—"starving student" status. He told me, "I got the full advance royalty; Dallas insisted that I keep it all." The book was published in 1984 as *In Search of Guidance.* Dallas was forty-nine when he wrote it. (Interestingly, his first philosophy book, which he initiated and worked on for fifteen years, was published that same year: *Logic and the Objectivity of Knowledge.*)

In the introduction to the twentieth edition of Richard Foster's *Celebration of Discipline*, Richard cites the influence of Dallas's person and teachings on him. Dallas and I attended a Quaker church and helped to call Richard there for his first pastorate. After writing *Celebration*, Richard recommended to Harper that Dallas write a theology of the disciplines that Richard had heard him teach. Dallas had named it "Exercise unto Godliness" [from 1 Tim 4:7 KJV], but the title became *The Spirit of the Disciplines.* Though Dallas knew all the material at some level, much of it required study and development. One can see from the footnotes and bibliography how many references he needed to organize.

I had been in churches and Sunday school classes and seminars where for about ten years Dallas had taught the material that was to become *The Divine Conspiracy.* I was especially impressed with Dallas's explanation that we couldn't understand *what* Jesus taught until we understood *the way* Jesus taught. I enjoyed sitting in the back row, watching people respond to the truth they were hearing. So often, as attendees left the room they would ask me, "Is this written anywhere?" So I encouraged Dallas to write down the material, but he couldn't seem to get to it. There was a particularly good set of audiocassettes made during an eight-week series at Hollywood Presbyterian Church in 1990. Armed with that album I said to Dallas, "If you don't write this, I'm going to." He later joked to others, "That got me going because I didn't want to live with an author."

Of course, I couldn't have written the book—I could only have transcribed the tapes. But neither of us knew how much would go into the birthing of that book. I believe Dallas said he rewrote the first chapter twenty times. When he showed me the initial draft of that chapter, I said, "It sounds like a musty old Christmas card." It was written in the style of his favorite seventeenth- and eighteenth-century authors. I'm usually not that "unkind," but God used it for good. I treasure this inclusion of me in Dallas's acknowledgments in the book: "Her loving patience, *insistence* and assistance have been . . . both incomparable and indispensable. This is her book."

In 1997 Dallas was invited to speak at the 90th Anniversary Celebration of Biola University. *The Divine Conspiracy* was now in the hands of the publishers, and I entered the auditorium that day thinking, "*Now* life can get back to 'normal.'"

I was sitting in the front row, and Dallas gave the first talk that I had heard on "The Disappearance of Moral Knowledge." It wasn't an emotional talk, but by the end, I had been moved to tears. It was a spiritual experience of God's depositing in me a knowing that a book had to be written on this information and that Dallas was the one who had to write it. I was applauding vigorously, and our eyes locked in the affirmation we recognized in each other.

Some time after that, Dallas agreed to be editor for a series of spiritual formation books for NavPress. I saw him writing something and inquired if he were working on the moral knowledge book. When he told me he had agreed to write a small manual-type book as the editor of the series, we had a bit of a tiff—because we were agreed that God had given him a previous assignment.

He assured me that this current project would be the sort of thing he could write very quickly. But Dallas is very thorough when he begins to put words to paper, and *Renovation of the Heart* required two years of writing time.

Though I had resisted his taking "time out" to write it, *Renovation* became my favorite book. I taught the DVD series in our church three successive years. Because of my decades as a therapist, my favorite chapters were 6 and 7, "Transforming the Mind," about thoughts and feelings. I even have a favorite sentence: "The single most important thing in our mind is . . ." Isn't that an attention getter? I have, since the late 1970s, used with my therapy clients what I call "imagery prayer," a type of inner healing. This favorite sentence stated what I had experienced with clients over many years: "The single most important thing in our mind is our idea of God and the associated images." This is followed by an A. W. Tozer quote, which Dallas had selected: "Our real idea of God may lie buried under the rubbish of . . . religious notions. . . . Only after an ordeal of painful self-probing are we likely to discover what we actually believe about God."[1]

I am very aware of the blessing of being in this house with forty-seven (of our fifty-seven) years of memories. As of this writing it has been six months since Dallas entered into the fullness of his "eternal destiny in God's great universe."[2] Often in these months the house has been a busy hub where friends and students have come to see Dallas's library and the place where he lived and wrote.

Many of us are attempting to sort through his class projects, lectures, speaking engagements, books, correspondence and so on. But when I am alone it's difficult to stay at any particular task because so often I come across some writing in a drawer or a paper placed in a book on a shelf, and I get caught up in the wonder and richness of his words. In our college days, I was very intentional before allowing my heart to fall so deeply in love with Dallas. I realized as a college senior that if I were to spend the rest of my life listening to my husband teach and preach, I'd better marry someone I valued hearing. I did!

It was God's amazing gift to two surrendered lives that we chose each other. We have, of course, weathered rough spots, but little did I know how much deeper and more expansive Dallas's teaching would become. Because of his books and his videos I will be able to go on listening to and learning from Dallas.

Living with the Great Thinker—and Feeler

- Becky Heatley -

I grew up in the home of a man who has been called "one of the great thinkers of our time." People often ask about what that was like, and expect to hear stories of great philosophical and theological discussions around the dinner table. But this great mind was cultivated on farms in the Ozarks during the Great Depression, blending in a unique sense of humor, humility, simple country wisdom and an ability to put up with just about anything. To give just one example, he told me that sometimes his family had onion sandwiches for lunch because there wasn't anything else to eat. I asked if the onions made him cry, and he said yes. "So what did you do?" I asked. "We'd just wipe away the tears and take another bite," he answered with a laugh.

Conversations in our home were often clever and humorous, *occasionally* getting rather deep. Both of my parents grew up in families that used humor to get through the tough times. And I mean *intelligent* humor. I think that was the beginning of the easy attitude my dad had about life.

Dad wouldn't let things like stress or insults or worries get to him. He didn't just brush them aside, but he was able to deal with them in an appropriate and joyful manner in the way he taught us to understand joy ("a pervasive and constant sense of well-being"). Even after the discovery of his cancer, as his body struggled through recovery from a major surgery and the effects of chemotherapy, his spirit maintained that sense of well-being as he told us he was just trying to learn whatever God wanted him to learn from this. With his love for hymns, I wish I had thought to tell him that he was a living example of "It Is Well with My Soul."

When I was four years old, we moved to a house in the rustic west end of the San Fernando Valley. The only other children near us belonged to a family with four boys. This was great for my big brother, of course, but a regular source of frustration for me. The boys put up with my presence as much as boys could, I suppose, but my memory of those early years includes many trips home on my tricycle in tears. Sometimes dad would come out and sit on the front porch with me and ask what had happened. I would unload my troubles right in his lap, and then he would say the magic phrase: "You know, when *I* was a little girl . . ." Of course, I knew he was *never* a little girl! But I would giggle and the tears would dry up as he told me a silly (sometimes fictional) story about his childhood. Whatever he intended to teach me at that moment, I was all ears.

You never knew what my father, "the great thinker," might say. When he was encouraging us to eat our vegetables he would say things like, "These'll make your cheeks curly." And as I grew older he became fond of greeting my friends with the question, "How's your copperosity?" I think he enjoyed watching young minds fumble with trying to come up with an answer for that.

Thinking was important. Think about *every*thing, don't just go along with what you're being told. "If you buy the car in that commercial," he'd say, "a beautiful woman will come and sit on your hood." Bill and I make the same kinds of comments to our daughter now. You can't just buy what they're selling—*think* about what's really going on there.

One of Dad's disappointments with the American education system over the last decade or so has been that students are arriving in college without having been taught how to think. They don't reason things out to a logical conclusion. They just buy what's being sold.

Popular music was a common teaching tool in Professor Willard's classes. Every few years a new song like "Dust in the Wind" or "Imagine" would be released, providing good material for philosophical discussions with college students. He took ideas that were being pumped thoughtlessly over the airwaves and challenged his students to think them all the way through. "Are we really just dust in the wind?"

We were driving in the car one day when I was fifteen and "Only the Good Die Young" was on the radio. Dad looked at me and said, "Does that mean that if you are good you will die young?" I don't think it took too long for me to reply that it was possible for me to be good and still live a long life. Later I even thought, "So if you are *not* good does that mean you *won't* die young?"

It was around that same time that I developed a habit of reading my Bible in bed before I went to sleep at night. My dad would occasionally come to my room while I was reading, having spotted an opportunity for brief conversations with his teenage daughter about God and other important things. Sometimes we talked about what I was reading, other times about the events of the day.

One evening I was worrying over something that was happening with my friends, and I wasn't sure what to do. Dad told me about a book called *In His Steps*, by Charles Sheldon. It's a novel about a group of church members who pledged that for an entire year they would not do anything without first asking the question, "What would Jesus do?" Dad said he often asked himself this question and advised me to do the same in this case. I soon read *In His Steps* and, while I didn't get to where I reviewed *every* decision under the lens of what Jesus would do, I considered it often.

About ten years later I was leading a high school girls' discipleship group that met at 6:00 a.m. every Friday. Our group read through *In His Steps* together and applied the "What would Jesus do" concept to our own lives. What would Jesus be like if he attended high school in 1990? How can we be like that? How can we model his behavior in our families and communities? It was thought provoking and challenging.

Another decade passed, and the WWJD bracelets and trinkets made their appearance. Many people wore these and gave them as gifts as daily reminders that turned their thoughts toward Jesus. WWJD quickly became a silly little catch phrase that most churchgoers knew, but few put any thought into it. People were joking about things like what kind of toothpaste Jesus would use, what kind of car he would drive and whether he would choose paper or plastic.

I asked my dad what he thought about the popularity of WWJD. "Well, it's good that so many people are asking that question," he said, as if at least they're heading in the right direction. But then he got a gleam in his eye as he said that now they need to move on to the more important question: "*How* would Jesus do it?" He said nothing further, but just left me to think about that. That was his way, of course—to acknowledge the good that is being accomplished and then give that little nudge to move on to the next step.

What an interesting thought! How *would* Jesus do it? I might be willing to do something purely because I know Jesus would do it, but can I do it *in the manner in which he would do it?* And how would I go about becoming the kind of person who naturally does what Jesus would do in the way he would do it? That takes us right back to the importance of thinking logically: I'll need to pick each activity (what would Jesus do?), define the manner in which it should be done (how would Jesus do it?), and identify the spiritual exercises necessary to help me become that kind of person. Needless to say, I'll be working on this for a while.

Oh, and I have occasionally heard the phrase, "What would Dallas do?" But let's please not ever go there. I mean, what would Dallas think?

Give 'em Heaven

- Larissa Heatley -

I am Dallas Willard's granddaughter, and he used to say I was a *grand*-daughter. But grand-daughters only exist with grand-fathers, and he was the best grandfather of them all. He always knew what to say, no matter what the issue was. He always knew what to do to make me feel better. Even if we were just playing games.

He would play the silliest games with me. There was one that wasn't really even a game, that I made up, and he played it every time I asked. We would go down my grandparents' driveway a little and sit on this big rock that was large enough that when I sat on it my legs would hang over the edge and just swing back and forth, and Grandpa would stand next to me.

The game of it was simply finding rocks and throwing them down the hill to see who could throw them the farthest. That was never really the main focus while we were down there; the main focus was whatever we were talking about. That is, at least until I wanted to talk about something else. I was young, so I don't remember what we would talk about. But I remember the way that we would talk. We would talk in any way that we wanted to. But he would talk in such a loving, calming way. He always talked like that.

I always wanted that voice to teach me at USC. Now I often think about how that isn't going to happen. But I've realized that he had already been teaching me more than I ever could learn in school.

He taught me how to learn and observe things without him saying anything.

He taught me the importance of thinking, and the importance of taking time to choose your words carefully.

He taught me the importance of the little things.

The little things that he did were my favorite. And the big things were my favorite too. It was just everything he did. It was so loving and kind and unconditional. He had unconditional love for every one that he met. That was another thing he taught me: love everyone. I need to work on that a little more. He had that one perfect.

Looking back, I see now that all the little things he did for me added up every day, one by one, and showed how much he cared. When he was in his study writing or typing on his computer I would often try to sneak up on him and scare him. He would always act surprised to make me happy. That is love.

He also used to wave us off when we drove away. Now some people will wave goodbye to their family for a little while, but he would wave at me from behind the white picket fence until we couldn't see each other anymore. He would do it every time without fail. It became our way of saying "I love you" and "see you soon."

"I love you" was the last thing I said to him. I will still see him soon in heaven. He told me in the hospital that if he passed it wouldn't be long until we resumed our life together.

The years to come without Grandpa will seem like nothing compared to the eternity that we will be spending together with the Lord, but it's already been too long without him here. It's been too long since I've held his strong, gentle, big, loving hands. It's been too long since I've had a hug from my magnificent, strong, larger-than-life, teddy bear, number-one Grandpa. It's been too long since I got wisdom from the biggest thinker I know.

I will always remember one sentence that really summed up everything he stood for and everything I need to do. He might not have meant it as anything, but I kept thinking about it. He said it to me in the hospital just before his last surgery. We were all walking out of the room and I was about to go sing with my youth choir at a homeless shelter. Grandpa called me back for a moment so we were the only two in the room, and he said, "Give 'em heaven." At the time I'm pretty sure he just meant it as a joke—or maybe he didn't. He had a way of saying something so meaningful without really knowing it. So anyway, "Give 'em heaven." That is what I plan to do.

The Joy of Working with His Hands

- John Willard -

While there is so much I could say about Dad and his life and influence on me, I'll use this space to present one of his facets that most people wouldn't know about: his healthy appetite for good, hard "common labor."

Dad had a lifelong zeal for physical work. It must not have been much more than a year before he left this life that he asked me to come over and give him a hand with replacing a long water pipe running from the house to a garden-hose tap that he'd installed years earlier. The pipe had rusted a little too much and started leaking, and there was a small patch of ground that was always wet. Dad wouldn't long tolerate that kind of waste, and he was the kind of man who took care of things like that with his own two hands and good sense. When I arrived he had already dug most of the trench by himself with pick and shovel. He let me finish the digging, then we strained together to turn and unthread the rusting piece and replace it. Then he lifted up his hands and declared, "That's it! We're done for today!" with evident satisfaction and gratitude.

He knew, or figured out, just about everything to do with household repairs, home remodeling, do-it-yourself projects, landscaping and growing food. Cutting back overgrown vegetation was a yearly necessity in a fire-prone rural area of the San Fernando Valley, and we always loaded up his little truck with our cuttings, stomping on the branches and brush to compact them in the bed between the two sideboards he had made out of four-foot by six-foot plywood boards by cutting notches to fit around the wheel wells. We would cover the load with a tarp and tie it down with ropes, then drive twenty-some miles to the landfill. Then we'd use pitchforks to push on one side of the top part of the load to make it fall off the other side, and pull the rest out over the tailgate.

Once or twice a year he would put a bandanna over his nose and mouth and crawl through the cramped crawlspace under the house to spray insecticide to keep Mom's kitchen from being overrun by ants.

Dad loved carpentry and built additions to houses, replaced staircases and window sills and floorboards, built his own book-shelves, and on and on. He felt great pleasure and even humble pride in the exercise of his skills to build with wood like Jesus the carpenter did. And of course, having spent a year in graduate school working full time as a roofer, he never hired anyone to do any roofing or reroofing work but always did it himself, usually with me as his helper. The last roofing he did was a complete reshingling of my sister's house, and Becky and Bill and even young Larissa were up on the roof with us hammering nails.

He took joy in such labors. In part that was purposeful—one more avenue in which he could put into practice his good-spirited eagerness to live as our Father would have us live, working joyfully unto the Lord. And I'm sure he wanted to be a good role model for me in that respect, because he was always admonishing me to find the enjoyment in labor. He urged me to discover how a person can ignore the dust he's breathing and the cuts he's getting, being too filthy, hot and thirsty, and the aching in his muscles, and just con-centrate on doing the task (and it works, too!).

But in part Dad's love for industrious exertion was just a natural upwelling within him. Later in life he would often tell me that it had been too long since he'd done any good physical work, and he missed it (though he had to limit himself, because an afternoon of hearty, sweaty toil could result in a following day of being too sore to concentrate on writing a book or preparing for classes and speaking engagements).

Once, the man who lived next door found he had a heart condition and decided he wanted to sell his house and land for a very low price—if he could get it all in cash—so he could go and "see the world." Dad didn't want to get involved in a transaction that might be taking advantage of his neighbor's situation, but after a few months when no buyers were to be found the man asked again if Dad couldn't help him out. So Dad took a loan to get the cash, bought the property and rented out the house. Before too long he and I began building a small two-bedroom, two-car-garage house on the big empty area that the man had used as a little chicken ranch.

Dad hired surveyors, a professional plumber to get the piping laid out, another neighbor to pour and finish the foundation, a framing contractor with a crew to get the frame up fast and an electrician for the basic wiring. But we did everything else ourselves.

On many occasions a friend or a few friends of his, some of them his students, would help us for a day or two on building projects. And Mom and Becky were called on to help many times in many ways. I remember Mom making preserves from plums he harvested and getting honey from his beehives into jars, and young Becky gathering eggs from his chickens and preparing vegetables from his garden. Dad loved manual labor most of all when it was in fellowship with friends and family.

I hope and expect that Dad's intellectual achievements as a philosopher and theologian will live on through the ages, and be amplified in the work of others who follow after him. I have faith that he'll be remembered for his graciously giving, Christlike love for people. But I think an accurate portrayal of my father has to include his enjoyment of physical labor and his belief that it is usually an important part of the good life that God wants for his children.

Dad was the person I relied on, whose opinion I cared about more than anybody else's, whose perceptions of the world were central to my own, who taught me to question authority and convention and to be committed to my own well-formed beliefs in spite of what others might think of me. Dallas Willard stands as a shining example of a faithful husband, father, friend, pastor, teacher and neighbor—doing everything with a good spirit and living a completely unselfish life, turning a deaf ear to personal ambition, not seeking after a big income but trusting God to make him adequately prosperous, resolute in being content with frugality, and always self-sacrificingly focused on working diligently toward the accomplishment of his too-numerous difficult undertakings. A precious, wonderful, loving person with complete integrity, honesty and commitment to goodness. I miss him more than I can bear.

A Word from a Different Reality

Jan Johnson

I couldn't believe it. The keynote speaker was admitting to everyone that he had wanted to be the best of the five keynote speakers. Why was this strange man saying aloud things I had wished, probably everyone had wished, but never admitted to anyone?

Then things got even stranger. He explained that he had figured out that what he needed to do was pray for the other four keynote speakers. So, he told the audience, he had prayed that each speaker would hear God well, communicate well and be received well.

This selfless, others-focused attitude went against everything I had been learning in the American Society of Journalists and Authors, an organization I had worked six years to earn the credentials to join. In that setting I was learning about how to promote myself. That couldn't be wrong, I thought, because the kind people in our local chapter helped me so much.

What was up with this guy on the platform at this event? I was mystified and somewhat disturbed. He was definitely a "word from a different reality."[1]

Later I looked at my conference booklet and noticed he was presenting a workshop called "How to Live One Day with Jesus." I
wondered if living just one day with Jesus would make me as odd
as this speaker was—but also, as obviously in sync with God as he
was. Was it possible that God wanted something better for me than
to be a so-called success?

INTRIGUED BY THIS DIFFERENT REALITY

After that 1991 Renovaré Conference, I began writing notes to
Dallas asking where he was speaking next in our area. A few years
later I showed up every night for his talks in Ojai, California. (A
week before he died he recalled one of those evenings. As I walked
in late, he said, he'd thought, *I know that woman with the silver
streak in her hair.*) He talked about the kingdom and how we can
live in the kingdom without anger and lust. He read Matthew 5:25
and said we could go to our accuser and ask, "What do you need
from me?" I was so terrified I could scarcely breathe. This was a
different reality. I felt like Butch Cassidy and the Sundance Kid who
kept looking back, seeing the lawman following them and saying,
"So *who* is this guy anyway?"

I reviewed my notes for days and finally wrote Dallas asking if I
could perchance have a look at the manuscript of the book he was
writing. Shortly after that I held in my hands chapters from a book
that would one day be called *The Divine Conspiracy.*

I tried putting this "living without contempt" approach into
practice. I saw that sarcasm was not being cute; the term is derived
from two words: *sarx* (flesh) and *chasma* (pit or gulf).[2] Sarcasm
creates a pit or tear or deep cut in someone's flesh. Why would I do
that ever again? I figured out that while irony was a beautiful thing,
sarcasm was irony with a knife twisted through it. But I objected
greatly to Dallas's statement that nothing could be done with anger
that couldn't be done better without it.[3] It would take years before
I agreed with that, but I was so fascinated with the idea that I kept

trying it out. Sure enough, I found I could "lay aside anger," as Dallas liked to say, and still get things done.

Soaking in these ideas and experimenting with them let their truth sneak up on me. Living without contempt didn't get me what I thought I wanted (to make my point!) but something better: I liked people more. It felt as if I was backing my way into the kingdom of God and "all these things" (love, joy, peace) were being added to my life. I worked through the Sermon on the Mount slowly, over and over again, using those chapters from *The Divine Conspiracy*. Between that and the gritty but lovely experience of twelve-step groups, I became (in the words of my husband) a different person.

Living in the Kingdom Here and Now

Soon I was not only practicing all kinds of spiritual disciplines, but also teaching and writing about them and helping directees with them in my work as a spiritual director. However, I didn't catch the idea that life in the kingdom is a "different reality" until I interviewed Dallas for *Discipleship Journal* in the later 1990s.

I'd left my office frustrated beyond belief from trying to transition from my beloved Compuserve account to Microsoft Outlook. No matter how I configured Outlook, it didn't work. I was in tears. I packed up my recording gear and headed to Casa Willard (Becky Heatley's name for Dallas and Jane's house). My editor had instructed me to specifically ask this question: What does it mean to be "ravished" by the kingdom of God?[4] When I asked, Dallas spoke of the availability of the kingdom of God right here and now.

Then he paused and drew a picture for me with words: "Let's say I'm a plumber going to clean out someone's sewer. You stay attentive to what you're doing at the moment. You ask, *How will I do this as Jesus would do this?*" (I knew he did his family's plumbing so I could picture him clothed as a plumber.) Another pause.

"If you encounter difficulties with people you're serving, or with the pipe or machinery, you never fight that battle alone." (Now I could see myself in my front yard looking at a hole in the ground with a broken mainline water pipe, almost in tears.) "You invoke the presence of God," Dallas said. "You expect to see something happen that is not a result of you!" Another pause.

"If you train yourself to thank God when these 'coincidences' happen, you'll see them as patterns in your life. The crucial thing is to be attentive to God's hand, not to get locked into thinking: *It's me and this pipe!* Never do that." Another pause.

Then he gave me one of his intense looks and said, "It's never just you and the pipe, Jan." I repeated back, "It's never just me and the pipe."[5] In my mind I continued, *It's never just me and Outlook.*

Through the years I have continued to relive that moment: it's never just me and my computer; it's never just me and an impossible writing project; it's never just me and this dinner I just burned; it's never just me and the homeless person dying in my arms. God never says, "Girl, you're on your own on this one." There is a kingdom. It is available to me. I can walk in it at any moment. Do I want it? Will I embrace it?

TEACHING THE KINGDOM

A few years after that Keith Matthews invited me to lead exercises in Dallas's Fuller Seminary class, "Spirituality and Ministry." In a conversation I had with Keith and Dallas, Dallas said he didn't plan to teach about the disciplines anymore. I asked him about this. Between the two of them talking to me that day, I saw that teaching disciplines is futile without teaching about the vision of life in the kingdom of God. It sets people up for rigidity and guilt. We need to be constantly reminded about life in the kingdom because it's such a different reality that we forget it. Dallas said something like this to me: "Everything you teach must be infused with that vision of life in the kingdom of God. We need to keep it in front of people."

I've tried to follow that advice, sneaking in the kingdom wherever possible. But even more I've tried to live in it, following what he showed me about living in the kingdom. That first year in the class I watched as students didn't seem to give him the respect he deserved. One asked me privately, "So does he even have a theology degree?" They seemed to smart off to him, but he not only didn't take it personally, he didn't even seem to notice. He answered their questions with great respect in a straightforward way. His choice to love others and his choice to do what God was urging him to do seemed to be untouched by others' attitudes toward him. He was living in the kingdom and doing just fine, even if I was appalled.

One time on a break at the Fuller class, I leaned over and asked him, "So do you *try* not to be a good speaker?" I know that sounds appalling but I wasn't being critical. This was an "ah ha" moment for me. I felt as if I finally got Dallas's kingdom approach.

Prior to the class I'd listened to some very old cassette tapes of his teaching in which he sounded like a sonorous Southern Baptist preacher vaunting the truths of the faith. But listening to him teach that day in class, I could see how he had changed. He wasn't trying to have flair, to impress anyone, or to convince anyone of anything. He understood my question—"So do you *try* not to be a good speaker?"—as genuine, and immediately he said, "Yes, Jan, I just *go and talk to people*, and let God deal with them."

Dallas had learned to cast off all efforts at "impression management." He didn't try to be eloquent. He disliked PowerPoint and thought it distracted from the human-to-human interaction that occurs between the speaker and the spoken-to. In that sacred interaction, no pushing oneself forward is allowed. After I told my husband and spiritual director what Dallas said, they both began saying to me as I went off to speak: "Just go and talk to people. You'll be fine." I don't have to try hard to do or be anything. No song and dance is needed. I just need to be available to the Spirit. I need to love the people in front of me.

My husband and spiritual director also frequently tell me, "Keep your hands behind your back. You'll be fine." That came from how I automatically put my hands behind my back after being with Dallas each year at the Fuller class. When I want to control a situation, speak up when it's better to be silent, or try to impress people as a speaker, I put my hands behind my back and it changes the atmosphere in my mind. I relax and pull back. I picked this up from watching Dallas walk around Mater Dolorosa (where the class was held) for two weeks with his hands behind his back. Putting my hands behind my back puts me in a teachable, listening frame of mind and I feel myself ease back into the space of the kingdom.

While I was usually on the receiving end of wisdom from Dallas, we often shared insights of the kingdom in ways that surprised me. For a while, he and Jane attended a particular support group my husband and I had been heavily involved in. It forced Dallas especially to look at how his actions played out and what might be changed.

One night, walking back to the car in the dark, he asked me how he could possibly do what the leader had suggested. "Well," I said, thinking of twelve-step wisdom, "it would mean abandoning outcomes. You do the right thing, but you can't control how others respond." He repeated after me, "abandoning outcomes," as if it were a foreign phrase. The look on his face asked, *Can a person really do that?* I felt such sympathy for him in facing this challenge, and we walked together in silence.

A few days later I spotted that phrase "Abandoning Outcomes" as a section heading in *Renovation of the Heart*.[6] We can teach truths, but we are all challenged to experience the life-giving nature of truth as we walk in it.

STAYING OUT OF THE WAY OF THE KINGDOM

Several years later, I was in a setting with Dallas where it was suggested that the students express their appreciation to him for his teaching. This "praise session" went on for two hours. After twenty minutes, Dallas began to hang his head. He wouldn't look up. After forty minutes, he looked up and said to the group, "What if I backslide? What then?" The students didn't know how to receive this; they decided he was kidding so they laughed. But I knew him well enough to know that he was truly frustrated. We talked of it later and he lamented the possibility that people might put their trust in him, not in the kingdom of God. He knew that idealizing someone can distract people from the major truths the person taught.

Some people chalk up his not wanting to be praised or highlighted to his modesty or having grown up in an earlier era. Others have thought he had a self-esteem problem. But this misses the point. Yes, it's appropriate to thank God for speaking to us through another, and it's okay if the person hears that. But lifting people up with gushing praise imitates our culture of celebrity and pushes out the kingdom dynamic. When we receive much from a teacher or leader or friend, the Spirit is at work and we need to thank God, not lift others up. This is the wisdom of the twelve-step phrase "principles before personalities." Our culture prefers the opposite: personalities above all else. (So much of what I learned from Dallas dovetailed exactly with what I heard in twelve-step; Dallas himself said that he would not trust a program of spiritual formation that did not significantly resemble Alcoholics Anonymous and its derivatives.)

Living in the Kingdom Now

This vision of life in the kingdom of God is, like Dallas, a word from a different reality. We get to lean into the kingdom minute by minute, as we do our work, love family members and pay close attention to whoever is standing in front of us. This divine conspiracy is a great adventure.

We don't need to shore ourselves up; we really do have everything we need (Ps 23:1). We don't need to impress each other; we
are well-loved and much-delighted in. God really is enough.

Jan Johnson is an author, teacher, seminary professor and spiritual director. She lives with her husband in Simi Valley, California. Her most
recent book is *Abundant Simplicity* (InterVarsity Press). You can find
out more about her at JanJohnson.org.

4

The Beauty of a Virtuous Man

Keith Matthews

After thirty years of relationship with Dallas Willard, the impact he has left on my life is beyond words. Not only has his teaching been profoundly life changing, but equally so has been his person and character.

Early on I realized that Dallas's vocational life as a philosopher and his life of faith as a disciple of Jesus and a minister of the gospel flowed from the same source. Underlying virtue and integrity informed both his professional and personal life, and the embodied result was a kind and gentle man, brilliant in thought and generous in relationship with God and others. In other words, he was a walking example of a virtuous man. And the beauty of this radiated to everyone who knew him.

In his teaching and ministry Dallas often offered a prayer for those who were gathered:

My prayer for you is that you would have a rich life of joy and power, abundant in supernatural results, with a clear vision of never-ending life in God's world before you, and of the

everlasting significance of your work day by day. A radiant life
and a radiant death.

This turned out to be a prayer that formed him. These words could
not better describe his life, his teaching and his ministry.

My relationship with Dallas over these thirty years influenced
me in three major transitions and life phases. The first phase was
my early vocational search and eventual calling to pastoral ministry.
In this season of my life with Dallas I was the eager and overzealous
young seminary student and pastor, with more questions and more
frustrations than he probably was ready for. And while he would
never own the role of mentor or use that type of language, he certainly filled that category. Dallas resisted this type of relationship,
though he was asked by countless people to be their mentor. Part
of his mentality came from his view that Jesus would do the direct
mentoring (discipling), free of human dependence. Another factor
was simply his humility, his view that he was not really worthy of
being called a mentor, though many would give him this mantle.

In phase two, I fell into the position of being Dallas's colleague—
though never his equal, from my point of view. I was in awe of his
brilliance and for many years felt inadequate or unworthy to be
identified with interpreting his ideas. Yet he loved me all the same
and never made me feel less than his partner in ministry.

In phase three, I found myself in loving friendship and support
to Dallas, caring for and advising him on his advisory team and
partnering in the Renovaré Institute. This era holds many sweet
memories of meetings, dialogues and times together talking about
Jesus, our families and always about ministry and the kingdom.

Teacher and Mentor

As a young aerospace engineer and budding seminary student I met
Dallas Willard in the summer of 1984, somewhat by accident. In the
early days of our married life, my wife Christa and I were attending

a large southern California church. Every year one of the veteran Sunday school classes would invite a guest speaker for the summer. The leader of this class approached me one Sunday morning and with great excitement invited my wife and me to attend the class. He said a very special speaker would be joining us, a professor from USC. So we, along with many others, walked into a packed Sunday school room bracing ourselves for what we hoped would be some good teaching. Little did I know what I was in for, but the result was nothing less than a paradigm shift in my Christian understanding.

In those twelve weeks my Christian experience seemed to go from black and white to high-definition color. Each Sunday morning I sat with eager anticipation in this class listening to a gentle and wise professor speak about "Guidelines to Life in the Kingdom of God." He spoke about God not in grand propositions with scriptural add-ons, but with a depth of experience and insight that I had rarely heard from any Christian leader. His demeanor and delivery of content could only be described as "old school," meaning that it was without any theatrics or attempt to manipulate his hearers. He was a classic lecturer.

But there was something different about him. He spoke softly, but with great precision, often closing his eyes and even tearing up with quiet emotion over the beauty of his content and descriptions of the kingdom life. It was as if he was speaking of another land, a magnificent and beautiful place that he knew well and was inviting us into. This class began a personal adventure with Jesus like I had not known previously.

Prior to meeting Dallas, my Christian experience was formed around three radical Christian movements that set the DNA of my faith and life, which eventuated in my attending Fuller Theological Seminary and becoming a pastor. As a product of the southern California "Jesus Movement" of the early 1970s, I cut my teeth on a revivalistic form of Christianity that was passionately concerned with a few basic things: (1) Go all out for God now, because he might return at any moment, and (2) People need to be evangelized—right now! (3) So get after it!

Dallas's teaching over the twelve weeks of class became for my wife and me a paradigm-shifting experience. He spoke with a sense of authority and clarity about Jesus and discipleship that I had not heard before. It matched my radical past but grounded it not only in Scripture but in a logical theological perspective for living life, now! Dallas convinced me that the gospel was not just about getting people forgiven and bound for heaven, but "an invitation to a life in Jesus, where I am learning from him how to live my life as he would live my life, if he were in my shoes."

And Dallas convinced me that discipleship *is* the basic entrance into faith, not an advanced option, and that a profoundly transformed life is available now *in this life*, not just the next. I also began to understand that spiritual disciplines are a means of grace and growth, placing me in God's presence whereby I can be changed into his likeness; they are not meritorious actions that soon turn to legalisms. These truths and many more opened a whole new world to explore and experience. Yet while these teachings were so profound in reordering my Christian DNA, there was something else that affected me as well.

It was Dallas the person—not just the teacher, theologian, philosopher or brilliant thinker, but who he was, what he was, how he interacted and gave of himself to me and to others. In my early years of interacting with Dallas this was always the case—profound theological ideas delivered through profound modeling in his life. In an age of celebrity pastors and leaders, nothing could be further from Dallas's aspirations than being a star. Perhaps his humble upbringing and his own life with Jesus really grounded him in a different model of leadership.

I remember that shortly after meeting Dallas I gave him a seminary paper I was proud of, hoping to impress him or at least to incite some conversation on a problem I saw as important. The paper was titled "A Kingdom Summons to Simplicity and Frugality in an Age of Riches and Affluence." Sounds good, doesn't it?

Dallas kindly took the paper and returned it to me the next week. I couldn't wait to see what he thought. The paper was filled with many red marks and comments, very teacher-like. At the end of the paper he wrote, "You've written about some very important things in this paper. . . . Let's spend some time thinking together about this paper, and see if there is more to consider or learn. OK?"

At the time of this discussion he was writing *The Spirit of the Disciplines*, so he gave me a fresh copy of chapter ten in the book, "Is Poverty Spiritual?" This chapter related to the paper I gave him, which in many ways reflected my bias against being rich and essentially exalted a ministry of poverty (perhaps too much Tony Campolo and Ron Sider in those days for me!). With gentleness and love Dallas showed me that "being poor was the least effective way of helping the poor," and that the gospel was "just as much for the up and in, as it was for the down and out." The gospel must be all inclusive! This example shows the kind of mentoring that formed my twenty-five years of pastoral ministry, which fueled my passion for Christlike transformation for those in the local church and the seminary. This story also reflects a key aspect of Dallas's formation in Christ: being radically generous with his time. He was not the disengaged, distant professor but an available, kind and caring teacher. His generosity with time was very profound for me and for so many.

Collaborator and Colleague

At the time I was finishing my doctorate, my friend Jim Smith was working with Dallas as his assistant in his doctor of ministry class at Fuller Theological Seminary, titled Spirituality and Ministry. Jim decided to pursue an additional graduate degree, so I ended up being Dallas's assistant teacher for the class—and then for seventeen years.

The uniqueness of the class was that it was held for two weeks in a monastery setting. We ate together, slept in our monastic rooms together, lived in deep community for those weeks. Pastors from all over the world came to listen to Dallas teach. Pastors who were broken, tired and weary from ministry. Pastors looking for hope and possibility to keep going. Pastors who wondered if this Christlike transformation was really possible. And who also wondered, was this Dallas Willard guy for real?

Class after class, without fail for twenty-seven years, students came and got what they were looking for: they tasted Jesus and his kingdom in profound and personal ways. They received healing and hope for what could be in their congregations—and I got to watch it happen. What a privilege!

In the early years I was so nervous in my role. What could I say to add to Dallas's profound insights? Both Jim and I realized that our best role was to watch the students' faces during Dallas's powerful lectures, and when their eyes glazed over with quizzical awe at some profound thought, to stop Dallas and say, "Dallas, could you please say that again? I think that thought just floored us."

As time went on I would jump in with some of my own lectures, which became my take on Dallas's teachings. Dallas was so kind and encouraging. I'm sure there were times that I said some things he didn't agree with, but he never made me feel less than a colleague, and he assured me that I really did have something to say.

After spending so many years working with this same class, one would wonder, did it ever get old or too repetitive? Never! Dallas had a way of saying the same thoughts with just a subtle change of words, or he would rabbit trail, sharing an experience that brought deeper insight to his topic. These moments were the best, not knowing where he would go or what he would say. They often produced some of the most sacred moments of the class. One could sense the kingdom breaking in upon us in a very special way.

Once in a great while a student would challenge him on his thoughts or ideas, and he would quietly and calmly respond: "I certainly may be wrong in my thinking here, I have much to learn from all of you, but all I would ask is that you think about it and 'try out' in experience what I am saying." He modeled the virtue of Christian civility over and over again in the years I was with him. I never saw him lose it, never saw him get angry. It just wasn't in him. He would often say, "Anything done in anger can be done better without it!"

Another of Dallas's sayings that I think of often in my own ministry in the church and the academy is "Seek not to speak, but that you might have something to say." Pastors and professors are paid to give our thoughts and opinions, often to our own peril or pride. But Dallas's haunting question was, Where do these thoughts and opinions come from? The answer is always that they come from an inner person, from a formed character. And this answer calls us to further ask, What kind of person am I becoming?

For Dallas, a life in God was an experiential relationship, not propositional ideas or facts. Our teaching can't help but flow out of who we are. As he would often read from 2 Corinthians 2:15-16, "For we are to God the aroma of Christ among those who are being saved and those who are perishing. To one we are the smell of death; to the other, the fragrance of life" (NIV 1986).

Not only did this idea of having something to say affect Dallas's own teaching, but it affected the way he *delivered* his teaching. At first glance one might say Dallas's style was just "old school"—a-stand-behind-the-podium, no-frills lecturer. That may be true, but there was more to it. Dallas rejected the thought of manipulating his audience through a technical style or theatrical mode. He believed that if you had a message that was thoughtful and true and birthed and bathed in prayer, God would bring the effect needed, in the way people needed it. In other words, he trusted God to bring about the *power* in his message. I witnessed this truth over and over again. No flash, no frills, just a simple presentation, well-prepared and thoughtful, but wow! The power of God came!

One portrait of how deep this effect was on his hearers is from an experience I had at one of the churches I pastored. Dallas came to my church to share a three-day seminar. On the second day a college student approached him after one of his talks and asked if they might have lunch together to talk about his ideas. Dallas graciously said yes. At lunchtime they grabbed a prepared box lunch and sat together on some steps at the side of the stage. What began as a private conversation, just the two of them on the stairs, turned to a slow but steady trickle of people surrounding them, literally leaning in to hear Dallas's thoughts shared with the young man.

By the end of lunch thirty to forty people were listening in, hoping to catch another powerful thought. It was an amazing sight. I remember starting to tear up, watching the power in the moment, seeing the hunger of the people to hear Dallas's wisdom. I have witnessed this scene countless times over the years. Dallas expected God to produce such great effects, but didn't trust his own abilities or manipulation to bring them about. He taught me this and I can bear witness that it's true.

One of Dallas's most popular sayings about the human self is this: "You are a never-ceasing spiritual being with an eternal destiny in God's great universe." Dallas witnessed in Jesus' ministry the power of "one person at a time." This is why Dallas modeled love and dignity to those who approached him. I have seen him minister for hours at a time, and even in his tiredness still give his time and attention to the person right in front of him. In the years I taught the Fuller class with him, over and over again students shared with me how valued and important Dallas made them feel. He looked them in the eye, took them by the hand, listened to them, prayed for them, told them they make a difference in the kingdom of God. This was as much a ministry of Dallas as was his speaking and writing.

Friend

In the summer of 2008, Dallas and I took on a big assignment. Little did I know what we were in for. We taught our usual two-week class at Fuller in June, but then decided to accept an invitation to teach "down under." We were off to Australia for another two-week class for the Australian College of Ministry (ACOM). Although we were a bit tired from our previous class we felt that this was God's timing for a big trip that might never happen if we didn't go then.

But a problem hit us just weeks before we were to leave. Dallas was working at his home clearing weeds and brush, and he noticed some trimming that needed to be done on top of an old shed. It was around ten feet high, so this old roofer (as a young man he was a trained roofer) got on top of the shed and started trimming away. But something happened. He was reaching too far to cut some brush and found himself falling off the shed onto an old barbecue (which thankfully broke his fall). He was in great pain, but hobbled into his house and then to the doctor, where x-rays revealed he had a slight fracture in his pelvis. He would be on crutches for the better part of a month.

Dallas's wife, Jane, was very concerned about the upcoming trip, wondering if it was even possible for him to go. But Dallas was fully committed and it was decided that we would press forward in spite of his condition. Jane said to me with deep concern, "Please take care of him and make sure he's safe." My role increased beyond my normal concerns for Dallas and the class itself. I needed to make sure he made it back home without further injury. The demands of the trip would take a toll on most healthy people, let alone a freshly injured one.

The crutches proved difficult to manage, yet gave Dallas a small sense of stability. But not me! How would he traverse stages and podiums? How would he handle the retreat terrain? How would he even get into and out of the shower? I was on high alert for the whole trip, waiting for something to happen. Yet Dallas was calm and kind, even with the pain he was daily enduring.

For the first few days in Sydney we were at a large church giving lectures open to the public, before the class was to begin a few days later. Right away I noticed the carpeted steps up to the podium, a couple of feet above the floor level. I thought, *keep your eye on his every move.* Day one was amazing—we had great connection with people and God's presence was evident. Day two arrived and things were going well. Dallas was tired but faithful, as always. When he finished his last lecture he sat down on the stage and talked with a few people who had questions. I stayed close by and talked with some local pastors, but then realized I had turned my back on Dallas.

When I turned around he was just getting ready to step off the carpeted stage when he caught a crutch at the top level. At that point I was twenty feet away, and it felt like I was watching a movie scene in slow motion. Down the stairs he went—with a perfect face plant at the bottom. Horror was my only response. *Oh no, is he okay? How could I have let this happen? Will this be the injury that sends him to the hospital or worse?*

Thankfully he was coherent, but now in more pain, with a large contusion on the side of his face. All I can say is that Dallas was a tough man. We got him the needed medical attention and by the evening he was doing better. Nevertheless, the rest of the trip I was on even higher alert.

Even with the challenges that Dallas faced, his ministry was a model of faithfulness and love. He loved to minister to pastors and Christian leaders. He had a high sense of responsibility to fulfill his calling to Jesus and his kingdom. When we arrived at the retreat center for our weeklong class in the "blue mountains" of Australia, our very rustic rooms shared a common, very thin wall. Each morning when I would hear Dallas's shower going next door I'd pray, "Lord, please protect my dear friend from injury." And then the water would go off and I would hear the most beautiful thing: Dallas's lovely baritone voice singing hymns, one after another, praising and loving God.

Difficult situations can bring out many things in people. Like the trip to Australia, cancer didn't reveal the worst of Dallas but the best of him. I will miss the many conversations about joys and challenges, family and friends, about theology and philosophy, and how Jesus is in all of it. But most of all I will miss my beloved friend, who more than anyone in my life embodied the beauty of a virtuous man all the way to the end. "A radiant life and a radiant death!"

What can we learn from this virtuous man? Really, it's quite simple. Believe and trust Jesus, his invitation and that his processes have a proven and transformative result. Seek to be the kind of person who loves people one at a time, face to face, and watch for Jesus to produce the fruit. Be faithful and intentional every day; the kingdom is on the move and we are invited in on it. Finally, think magnificently of God—always!

Dr. Keith J. Matthews is chair of the Graduate Ministry Department and professor of spiritual formation and contemporary culture at Azusa Pacific University.

PART TWO

Philosopher and Professor

The USC Service

On October 4, 2013, a gathering of approximately 120 individuals sat in the Caruso Catholic Center at the University of Southern California. The sanctuary was lined by warm wooden panels and decorated with religious statues and images. As one of the speakers would later observe, the setting seemed most fitting. Images of Teresa of Ávila and Augustine looked down from the walls, the beatitudes could be seen behind each speaker and the last two words from a tapestry over the doorway read "follow me."[1]

While this was the only one of the three tributes to Dallas orchestrated by those who had known him best as an academic philosopher, it was the one that I found most deeply moving. Those who presented had observed Dallas's daily life as a professor, colleague, dissertation chair, department head and secular writer. Most of those present had not seen him flipping skillfully through a well-worn Bible, or heard him talking about life in the kingdom of God, or listened to his baritone voice singing a gospel hymn. Yet each had observed his life, a life lived in a radically different, wonderfully warm and inviting way.

Scott Soames, distinguished professor of philosophy, worked with Dallas for more than four decades. He hosted the gathering and reminded those attending that Dallas was, for many years, "the teacher with the greatest range in the School of Philosophy, regularly teaching courses in logic, metaphysics, ethics, aesthetics, history of ethics, philosophy of religion, and the history of philosophy from the seventeenth through the twentieth century, including both sides of the twentieth-century split between analytic philosophy and phenomenology." Soames also pointed out that Dallas had chaired thirty-one successful USC dissertations in philosophy, the last in 2007, and from 1982 to 1985 had served as director of the School of Philosophy.

In scholarship, those attending this service knew Dallas Willard as an expert on the German phenomenologist Edmund Husserl. Dallas published his own book on Husserl in 1984. According to Soames, it was reviewed in the *Philosophical Review, Husserl Studies, Philosophy and Phenomenological Research, Review of Metaphysics* and the *Journal of the British Society for Phenomenology*, and it remains a standard reference in such venues as the *Stanford Encyclopedia of Philosophy*.

Kevin Robb spoke from the perspective of being with Dallas at USC for each of Dallas's forty-seven years in the philosophy department. Dallas's appointment was the first Robb voted on, and, he said, it was the single most important vote he cast because of the significant impact that Dallas had on the School of Philosophy, "more so than any professor during that time frame."

One by one, voices were heard from those who knew Dallas Willard in ways unobserved by most of his friends in the Christian world.

Ara Astourian, a student, recalled how Dallas respected and treated him as one of his peers. "To put it in [Dallas's] terms, though he knew we weren't equally worthy, he believed we were of equal worth, and acted toward me as though that were true." Ara's voice broke when he said that Dallas called him his friend, and that this was the greatest honor he had ever known.

Kenny Walker was one of the thirty-one students whose dissertations were chaired by Dallas Willard. His beautiful and lasting impression of Dallas is the image of him standing with one arm connected to a source of purified and purifying power and the other arm stretched out to anyone who might wish to take his hand and partake of that goodly power themselves.

A very special part of the program concerned a book manuscript that Dallas was trying to finish before he died. Three former doctoral students under Dallas, whom Dallas chose to complete this manuscript—Gregg Ten Elshof, chair of the Department of Philosophy at Biola University, professor Steve Porter of Biola University, and Aaron Preston, chair of philosophy at Valparaiso University—presented on the book, *The Disappearance of Moral Knowledge*, Dallas Willard's magnum opus.

Scott Soames concluded the discussion of Dallas's manuscript by quoting words on this subject, found by Aaron Preston, that Dallas wrote in 1971.

> Although there are . . . senses in which wisdom and virtue cannot be taught, the university which set itself to trade in humanly important truths of all sorts . . . may contribute to its student becoming *wiser* if not wise. . . . A humanely responsible program of . . . education would lead the student into a vivid awareness of what can be done in *his* probable life circumstances by intelligent cultivation . . . of the physical, . . . conceptual, emotional, social and moral powers of the human being. It should, thus, teach the truth, including the truth about *how to get at* the truth. . . . Were the university . . . to undertake such a task, it would find millennia of human experience ready to yield testable hypotheses. There are even some wise people . . . still alive today.[2]

Soames then stated, "Those words, including the final poignant line, remain as powerful today as they were when Dallas wrote them, despite our loss of one of the wisest among us."

He closed the tribute with these words: "He was, quite simply, that Professor of lore who students hope to find but don't really expect to—the one who enriches their lives by getting them to see more in themselves, and in life itself, than they had imagined."

As you can observe from this description, so many of Dallas's former students and colleagues could have written beautifully in this section if space permitted. In the chapters that follow you will hear from three of Dallas's former PhD students, Greg Jesson, Steve Porter and J. P. Moreland, and one former undergraduate student, Brandon Paradise, whose lives were deeply impacted by the philosopher Dallas Willard. Gary Black Jr. was also shaped by Dallas's teaching, and Eff Martin, Quinton Peeples, Gayle Beebe, John Kasich and John Ortberg represent Dallas's influence in various fields beyond the university.

THE EVIDENTIAL FORCE
OF DALLAS WILLARD

Steve L. Porter

An interesting thing about Dallas Willard is that, if you are a good student of his work, you should neither give him too much credit nor too little credit for the kind of person he was and the sorts of things he accomplished. What I mean is this: Dallas taught that the ultimate goal of human existence is to receive life from above—the reign of God—and allow that divine life to so permeate our thoughts, attitudes, beliefs, desires and powers that who we are and what we are able to do is beyond what could be accomplished by our own natural abilities alone.[1] This is life constantly enlivened by the kingdom of God. So when we reflect on Dallas's life and ministry, we should say: "Wow, look what God can do in and through a person who is utterly abandoned to him." This is to look through, even past, Dallas and credit the empowering presence of Jesus as the ground and living source of who Dallas was and what he did.

On the other hand, Dallas was such a unique conduit of life from above. He had come to be so permeated and influenced in his thoughts, attitudes, beliefs, desires and powers that he stood out like a city set on a hill. No doubt this was all by grace. Dallas did not deserve to be allowed into such a life. But he did, of course, have something to do with it. In this sense, Dallas's teaching and writing is equally clear: human persons have a role to play in receiving life from above and allowing that life to permeate and influence their own. Dallas received and allowed the Spirit of Christ to work in his life perhaps more effectively than anyone I have ever known. Receiving and allowing in practical and bodily ways is what Dallas referred to as spiritual disciplines.

It is no surprise that Dallas took the disciplines seriously in his own life. This seriousness is not seen so much in the intensity of his practices, but in how embedded the disciplines were in Dallas's daily affairs. For instance, as many will attest, Dallas made it a habit to hum hymns throughout his day. Another practice was to put his hands behind his back when people would question him as a reminder to listen and be gentle in response.

I remember at a Theological and Cultural Thinkers (TACT) gathering someone asked Dallas what the most significant discipline was in his own life. I leaned forward in my seat to make sure I heard Dallas's response. Would it be contemplative prayer, *lectio divina*, fasting, extended periods of solitude? Dallas responded: Bible memorization. For Dallas, memorizing Scripture was no legalistic, merely cognitive enterprise. As New Testament scholar Mike Wilkins once said to me, "I have never met anyone who has a more intuitively immediate grasp of the actual meaning of Scripture than Dallas Willard." As Dallas memorized the text, he interpreted and applied it, allowing the Spirit of God to breathe the life-giving, nourishing meaning of the Word of God into his heart/spirit/will. For Dallas, Bible memorization was a dynamic process of harmonizing his will with the will of his Father.

I recall a time in Dallas's office at USC when I asked him what disciplines he practiced. He was a bit reluctant to share too many specifics. He had the reasonable concern, I think, that I might simply take on his practices without taking on the overall approach to the spiritual life that gave birth to his specific practices. Eventually he gave me an example of one of his disciplines. Perhaps he knew it would sound so odd to me—that it was *so peculiar to him*— that I would never be tempted to mimic it. Dallas shared that as he drove his car he imagined Jesus on the cross on his left side and the empty tomb on his right side (or it might have been the other way around). I have absolutely no idea what that practice did for Dallas, but I am struck by the reality that he drove back and forth from south Los Angeles to Chatsworth hemmed in by the death and resurrection of Jesus. And while I have never practiced that discipline myself, Dallas's sharing of it did help me to realize that it does not matter much what particular disciplines we engage in as long as we have the underlying intention to draw near to God and his kingdom resources in effectual ways.

It is interesting to note that of the 265 pages of *The Spirit of the Disciplines*, only 35 pages actually address specific disciplines (about 13 percent of the book). Most of the book develops a theological and psychological framework that motivates engagement with God in whatever ways best suit our own circumstances and personality.

My appreciation for Dallas was actually slow in coming. It escapes me now whose sky-blue, clothbound copy of *The Spirit of the Disciplines* I borrowed in the summer of 1990, but as I read it I was writing angry comments in the margins—in ink! I was reading as a recovering legalist, and I am afraid that all of Dallas's talk of the disciplines went straight into my all-too-recently vacated categories of legalistic Christianity. I was twenty years old at the time, and much of what I wrote in the margins contained the colorful prose of an angry, disillusioned young man who only saw in Dallas's words more hoops to jump through to try to get God to like me. Reading *The Spirit of the Disciplines* was, at that time, further evidence to me that either Christianity did not possess any unique mechanisms of spiritual change (it was just another version of legalistic willpower fueled by shame and guilt) or, more bleakly, that Christianity simply was not true. The irony of my initial response to *The Spirit of the Disciplines* is that it would be that very book that, paired with the evidential force of Dallas himself, helped bring me back around to a firm confidence in Jesus and his way of personal transformation.

THE COST OF NON-DISCIPLESHIP

When we look at the pages of the New Testament, we are struck by the qualitatively good life that Jesus commends to those who follow him. Jesus says that if we come to him and take his yoke upon us, we will find easy rest; that if we abide in him as he does with us, we will enter into fullness of joy; that worry no longer needs to be an issue as we seek first his kingdom; that if we continue in his teachings, we will know his truth and be set free from enslavement to sin; that there is a way to love God with our whole being and to love everyone around us as well. Paul, of course, continues and exemplifies this theme, proclaiming that the kingdom of God is righteousness, peace and joy in the Spirit; that the Spirit of God has poured the love of God abroad in the core of our beings; that there is a way to be content in any circumstance; that we can allow Christ to strengthen us in the face of hardship and death; that the outcome of living with the Spirit is love, joy, peace, kindness, patience and the rest.

It would be one thing if Jesus and his earliest followers taught these ideals as extrinsic commands that Christians should do their level best to live up to: try really hard not to worry, work diligently at being joyful, do your best to find contentment, and when you fail at these things, try harder the next time. If that were the extent of formation in Christ, we would expect to find a lot of worn-out Christians, some doing better than others at living up to these ideals.

But Jesus and his friends do not teach these as extrinsic commands to be strived after on our own. Rather, they teach an *intrinsic* empowerment of the Spirit, constant interaction with whom is meant to enable persons to actually reach these heights. As Ezekiel expresses it, "I will put my Spirit in you and move you to follow my decrees and be careful to keep my laws" (Ezek 36:27 NIV). Or Paul says, "Walk by the Spirit, and you will not gratify the desires of the flesh" (Gal 5:16 ESV). On this point, Dallas writes that we can come

> *to count on,* to *expect,* that the Holy Spirit, God, Christ—the unbodily personal power that is the Trinitarian God—will act in my life to enable me to do the good and right in all things I am engaged with. . . . Jesus has arranged with the Father to give us a "Helper, the Holy Spirit, whom the Father will send in My name" (Jn 14:26). He will always be with us, and will direct and empower us, as we rely upon him and invite him into our activities.[2]

Despite my initial misinterpretation, Dallas is quite clear in *The Spirit of the Disciplines* that the disciplines are the means by which we invite the Spirit into our activities:

> My central claim is that we *can* become like Christ by doing one thing—by following him in the overall style of life he chose for himself. . . . We can, through faith and grace, become like Christ by practicing the types of activities he engaged in, by arranging our whole lives around the activities he himself practiced in order to remain constantly at home in the fellowship of his Father.[3]

Note that the disciplines are activities aimed at remaining in *constant fellowship* with the Father. Fasting, prayer, meditation on Scripture and the like are not transformative in and of themselves, but only as they attach the disciple to the transforming resources of the Godhead. Dallas goes on to write, "We *meet* and *dwell* with Jesus and his Father in the disciplines for the spiritual life."[4] Of course, we have a part to play:

Now that new life is graciously visited upon me, my part in
the redemptive process is to [submit myself to God]. God will
not do it for me any more than he did it for Moses or Elijah,
for his son Jesus or his apostle Paul. And if I do not submit my
actions through the disciplines that fit my personality, I will
not enter into the powerful, virtuous new life in a psycho-
logically real way.[5]

What I had somehow missed in my first reading of *The Spirit of the
Disciplines* is that submission to God through the disciplines is not
a meritorious work, but rather the disciplines are the means of
interactive relationship with God. It is essential for us to engage God
through them because that is simply how loving interaction with
another person works. Anything else wouldn't be loving interaction.

THE EVIDENTIAL VALUE OF SPIRITUAL MATURITY

So the Christian tradition proclaims that there are unique resources
available in Christ to bring about a transformation of our character.
When it comes to moral and spiritual maturity, Christians have
access to a transformational relationship with God that those
outside of Christ do not have in the same manner. If this claim is
true, we would expect the truth of it to be verified in our own and
others' experience. It would be reasonable to expect that our lives
would bear the marks of having been with Jesus (see Acts 4:13).
Dallas often spoke and wrote of the "verifiability" in Christian experience of the reality of spiritual life in Christ.[6]

And yet, what we often find are half-baked followers of Jesus,
myself as doughy as any of them. Perhaps I am being unduly
harsh on myself and on the earnest Christians with whom I am
most familiar, but how many of us can really say that our light
has shone before others in such a way that they see our good
works and glorify our Father who is in heaven (Mt 5:16)? Of
course, there are glimpses of that in our lives (we have our good

days and perhaps even good weeks), but far too often I find as much (if not more) evidence of spiritual immaturity as I do maturity. And then there are those occasions when we confront in ourselves or in another deep dysfunction, brokenness and darkness that causes us to question whether there has been any real change at all. G. K. Chesterton famously quipped, "There is only one unanswerable argument against Christianity: Christians."[7] Dallas thought it was right to expect that the truth of Christianity should show forth in the tangible lifestyles of Jesus followers, such that when it does not, that presents a reason to think that the claims of Christ are false.

This is not to say that Christians ought to be perfect, but that in the midst of our failures and brokenness we should be nonetheless making progress toward the upward call of Jesus to become like him. To the degree that we are making progress, we become a bit of evidence to the truth of Christ's claims. Jesus himself says of his called-out ones, "that they may be perfected in unity, so that the world may know that You sent Me, and loved them, even as You have loved Me" (Jn 17:23 NASB). Sheldon Vanauken puts it this way: "The best argument for Christianity is Christians: their joy, their certainty, their completeness. But the strongest argument *against* Christianity is also Christians—when they are sombre and joyless, when they are self-righteous and smug in complacent consecration, when they are narrow and repressive, then Christianity dies a thousand deaths."[8] To the degree that my experience of Christians (foremost myself) fits this negative description, Christianity "dies a thousand deaths."

THE EVIDENTIAL FORCE OF DALLAS WILLARD

This is where Dallas entered, stage right, in my life. It would have been one thing to read his books, to hear his teaching and to be eventually won over conceptually and theologically to the idea that Christianity truly does possess an understanding of change whereby human persons can become more like Christ. But Dallas did more than win me over conceptually and theologically. He was for me—and I daresay for any other person who encountered him—compelling evidence of the truth of Jesus' way. How disappointing it would have been if Dallas possessed a deep, penetrating analysis of Christian formation and yet himself turned out, once you met him, to be a rather lackluster individual. To be clear, Dallas was a very ordinary person in many respects—he certainly was not slick or polished. Rather, the evidential force of Dallas Willard was the extraordinary quality of his presence that emanated through an otherwise ordinary man.

Dallas testified to his own experience of encountering ordinary persons who had grabbed hold of life from above. After recounting his initial exposure to various spiritual writers (such as Madame Guyon, François Fénelon, George Fox, John Bunyan and John Wesley), Dallas writes,

> That these [writers] were, by and large, quite ordinary people only impressed me all the more that the amazing life into which they were manifestly led could be mine. I had been raised in religious circles of very fine people where the emphasis had been exclusively on faithfulness to right beliefs, and upon bringing others to profess those beliefs. Now that, of course, is of central importance. But when that process alone is emphasized, the result is a dry and powerless religious life, no matter how sincere, and leaves a person constantly vulnerable to temptations of all kinds.
>
> Therefore, to see actual invasions of human life by the presence and action of God . . . greatly encouraged me to believe that the life and promises given in the person of Christ and in Scripture were meant for us today. I saw that ordinary individuals who sought the Lord would find him real—actually, that he would come to them and convey his reality.[9]

Dallas's experience of these ordinary individuals greatly encouraged him in his faith, and he now stands in line with these Jesus followers who led amazing lives of deep inner goodness and love.

One of the more persuasive marks of his ordinary extra-ordinariness was the students and faculty at USC who were drawn to him even though they either knew nothing of his Christian commitment or if they knew, they did not share it. For instance, while I was a doctoral student at USC there was a steady stream of students who dropped by Dallas's office. Whenever he was at school, his office door was open. And whenever his door was open, he was rarely alone. And whenever someone was in with Dallas, there was often someone else sitting in the chair outside awaiting the next vacancy. And whenever there was someone in the chair, there were often two or three others hovering around the hallway or stairwell leading to Dallas's office to see if they might get a chance to be with him. I often wished Dallas had installed one of those number machines so that we could have taken a number and waited our turn.

It was odd enough that a professor of philosophy would be so sought after by his students, but in Dallas's case I came to discover that many of those visiting students were not studying philosophy. They were graduates and undergraduates studying literature, psychology, classics, engineering, law and so on. Once I realized that, I assumed that the majority of these students were Christians who had read Dallas's books and knew something of his reputation as a Christian leader. Maybe a parent or pastor had instructed them to meet Dallas while they were at USC. While I am sure that accounts for some of those who came, I was surprised to discover as I struck up conversations with those waiting in the wings that many had no clue that Dallas was a Christian, let alone a well-known Christian leader. They came, they often said, because they had stumbled in to one of Dallas's classes and they found his words, and his very person, compelling. They would come to talk with Dallas about the meaning of life, about emotional struggles, about painful losses they were experiencing, and he would listen and respond with wise and grace-filled words. This was an ordinary man who had become increasingly receptive to the grace of God, and it was contagious.

A Personal Adventure of Trust

In an article titled "The Three-Stage Argument for the Existence of God," Dallas lays out a way of assessing the evidence for God's existence. Toward the end of that article, Dallas writes: "Given the very best possible exposition, theistic evidences never replace a choice as to what kind of universe we would have ours to be, and a personal adventure of trust, which involves living beyond what we can absolutely know."[10] Such a personal adventure of trust in Jesus is precisely what Dallas did so well. As we give Christ the credit for who Dallas was and what was accomplished through him, we are grateful for Dallas and those like him whose lives stand forth against the backdrop of humanity as powerful evidence that Jesus is the way and the truth and the life:

> There was a "fullness of time" at which Christ could come in the flesh (Gal. 4:4), and there is likewise a fullness of time for his people to stand forth with the concrete style of existence for which the world has hungered in its thoughtful moments.... As a response to this world's problems, the gospel of the Kingdom will never make sense except as it is incarnated—we say "fleshed out"—in ordinary human beings in all ordinary conditions of human life. But it will make sense when janitors and storekeepers, carpenters and secretaries, businessmen and university professors, bankers and government officials brim with the degree of holiness and power formerly thought appropriate only to apostles and martyrs. Its truth will illumine the earth when disciplined discipleship to Jesus is recognized as a condition of professional competence in all the areas of life, since from that alone comes strength to live and work as we ought.[11]

Steve L. Porter (PhD, University of Southern California) is associate professor of philosophy at Talbot School of Theology and Rosemead School of Psychology (Biola University). Steve serves as managing editor of the *Journal of Spiritual Formation and Soul Care* and as associate director of Biola University's Center for Christian Thought. He lives in Long Beach, California, with his wife, Alicia, and their two children, Luke and Siena.

Moving Beyond the Corner of the Checkerboard

Greg Jesson

The Academic Checkerboard

On every checkerboard, if enough pieces are lost during a game, two corners of the board allow a trapped opponent to move back and forth ad infinitum, thus avoiding obvious defeat. To many, this perfectly describes the academic life. Once the possibility of discovering truth has been summarily abandoned, all that is left in the academic world is an ideological posturing that ensures a rich "research program" (in other words, provides sufficient material for conference participation and publications in respected journals) that will allow one to develop a detailed account of something that is, by design, irrefutable.

Of course, what is not immediately obvious is that whatever is by design irrefutable is also—by non-design—*utterly trivial.* Advanced education today, especially in the humanities, attempts in general and for the most part to not say anything about the world in which we live and the objective conditions under which human beings flourish. It is simply assumed that contemporary education has little—if not nothing—to do with practical concerns in life. (At most, a college education is seen to be practical only if it provides a passport "to get a good job.") However, the *infinitely practical* issue of what kind of character one has developed is rarely raised. Is one academically curious and honest, intellectually and emotionally insightful, historically informed, cognitively humble, and thereby radically empathetic? Curiously, one can receive an education at our best universities and never seriously think about any of these issues. It is often assumed that character is not a field of knowledge. As Os Guinness said in *Long Journey Home*, "The observation by Socrates in his trial that 'the unexamined life is not worth living' may be the most famous saying from the classical world—and also the least followed."[1] It is not irrelevant that contemporary institutions of higher education see themselves not as knowledge institutions, but as research institutions.[2] To paraphrase G. K. Chesterton, when people no longer believe in truth, they don't believe in nothing, they believe in research.

The thesis of this chapter is one simple and sharp point: *The heart of Dallas Willard's philosophical and religious works was that nothing is more practical and important to our lives than the possibility of being able to grasp (with adequate evidence) the nature of reality as it is in itself (i.e., knowledge).* The majority academic world, at least in the humanities, is opposed in principle to such a possibility; but in fact *any* rational defense that knowledge of reality is not possible necessarily and inconsistently depends on knowledge of some part of reality. Self-serving dogmatism is the only other option.[3]

Dallas took the words of the Old Testament prophet Hosea utterly seriously: "My people perish from lack of knowledge" (Hos 4:6).[4] In this light, Dallas gravely viewed the catastrophic state that is now upon us, in which the contemporary world has lost its belief in the existence of knowledge concerning the things that matter most. The personal and institutional consequences of dismissing the possibility of knowledge conveniently—at least for a while—allows one to do whatever he or she feels like doing. Moral and political obligation are seen as contingent, cultural norms as established by nothing more than historical accident. We could have believed otherwise.

Malcolm Muggeridge often said, "The only fish that goes with the stream is the dead fish." Dallas spent his entire life going against the swift stream of academic fads by seriously studying and defending the possibility of knowledge that grasps truths that are not simply part of one's own mind. For example, if I know that an aspen tree is in my backyard, or that the sun is ninety-odd million miles from the earth, or that the Pythagorean theorem is true, or that Abraham Lincoln was the sixteenth president of the United States, *what* I know is not part of my mind—they are all mind-independent facts.[5]

President John Kennedy once hubristically (and falsely) proclaimed that "All of man's problems are caused by man, and can be solved by man." However, after fifty years, almost every problem facing the world looks unfathomably convoluted and inexplicably unsolvable. This seemingly intractable situation is exactly what Hosea meant by people perishing for a lack of knowledge. This is the controlling fact in our world, and this is why everything turns on people's capacity to achieve an adequate degree of knowledge about our duties as human beings. As Dallas said, "What we assume to be real and what we assume to be valuable will govern our attitudes and our actions. Period."[6]

If grasping the nature of reality with adequate justification is not possible, then knowledge is not possible; and if knowledge is not possible, it is unclear exactly what the university is for. In contrast, Dallas saw that the pivotal issue in which *all* controversies finally culminate is the possibility of knowledge. Consequently, every investigation should begin with the question, "Are we talking about a field of knowledge or not?" Surprisingly, this is one of the most difficult questions to raise in the humanities today because the contemporary philosophical stream so powerfully and monolithically flows against it. (This question never gets raised in fields such as engineering, because either the airplane flies or it does not. Everyone is driven by the preponderance of the empirical evidence to hold that engineering is a field of knowledge. From this, of course, it does not logically follow that all evidence is empirical.)

Apart from exceptions for scientific fields, in almost every quarter of our civilized world knowledge and its closely related objective, truth, are ultimately considered a joke. Today, the person who claims to know something, who claims to have genuine wisdom about reality—especially about how people ought to live their lives—is often thought hopelessly naive, simplistic, uneducated, ethnocentric and old-fashioned. (Accordingly, Dallas said, "People don't like the truth because they want a little room to wiggle around in.") Ultimately, every view that denies the existence of truth and knowledge must—logically must—slip both elements back, however stealthily, into one's claims. Rejection of truth and knowledge simply presupposes some truth and knowledge.[7] Dallas often argued that people should be highly skeptical of any skepticism that holds knowledge is impossible. As he liked to say, "We should doubt our beliefs as well as doubt our doubts."

GREAT-HEART AND VALIANT-FOR-TRUTH

Like C. S. Lewis (and just as rare), Dallas could deftly uncover the ultimate issues on which an entire complicated controversy turned. He could argue powerfully for a point, weighing in with logic, history, fine distinctions, Scripture and the nature of one's own experience, but he never tried to force acceptance. He would constantly say things like, "This is how it seems to me, but you must examine the evidence yourself as you try to honestly and diligently search for the truth" (see Lk 10:26). This approach, equally rigorous and relaxed, allowed people to look at the relevant evidence and data for themselves without retreating into a debate and win-at-all-costs mode. Dallas wasn't interested in academic victories. He was interested in the truth. What else could explain his statement, "If Jesus knew of a better way to live than following him, I'm sure that he would be the first one to tell you to take it"?

Even more amazing was Willard's kindness. In his irrepressibly winsome and unassuming manner his acceptance of others, even when disagreeing, gently disarmed even the most severe critic. I remember how Richard Rorty was visibly moved by Willard's sensitive critique of his views when they participated in a dialogue on "The Question of Authority" at Stanford in 2005.[8] The closest I can get to succinctly describing Dallas is best captured in two characters from Bunyan's *The Pilgrim's Progress*: Great-Heart and Valiant-for-Truth. For a more contemporary comparison, if you can remember George Bailey in *It's a Wonderful Life*, the most generous and loved man in Bedford Falls (played by Jimmy Stewart), you are on the right track.

To get to the ultimate issues of life, Dallas posed four questions: What is reality? Who is well off or blessed? Who is a truly good person? How does one become a truly good person? How each person handles these questions will determine his or her "bane or blessing." More importantly, none of these questions are about that most sacred contemporary idol, feelings; each is about a realm of *knowledge*. Feelings and emotions are immensely important, but divorced from knowledge they are usually self-centered, myopic, insular and, ultimately, destructive. If that is the case, no one should be surprised to discover that the compass needle of their feelings almost always points to the magnetic north of themselves.

HOW IS KNOWLEDGE OF REALITY POSSIBLE?

In order to escape an all-embracing skepticism, which makes any serious examination of the four crucial questions impossible, Dallas knew it was necessary to establish how knowledge is possible. He realized, as most students in philosophy come to see, that the modern groundings of knowledge in Descartes, Locke, Berkeley, Hume and Kant fail to explain how we can come to know anything besides our own mental states.[9] All of these philosophers began by assuming that our awareness is always of some mental object such as an idea or perception, and not surprisingly, none can explain how it is possible to be directly aware of anything outside one's mind. In other words, given these philosophers' views, knowledge of a mind-independent world is impossible; and wherever knowledge is rejected, truth quickly becomes an intellectual casualty. *What Dallas came to see is that skepticism concerning the external world presupposes an account of the mind (an ontology of the mind) that makes knowledge impossible.* He arrived at this momentous conclusion by studying hundreds of philosophers, including Plato, Aristotle, Augustine, Thomas Aquinas, Francisco Suárez, Antoine Arnauld, Thomas Reid, C. E. M. Joad, G. E. Moore, Gustav Bergmann and Alonzo Church. However, the philosopher who had the greatest influence on Dallas's thinking was Edmund Husserl (1859–1938).

Even seventy-five years after his death, Husserl's significance to the intellectual climate of the twentieth and twenty-first centuries is hard to overestimate. Husserl had been a student of the immensely popular and innovative philosopher Franz Brentano (1838–1917). He was deeply influenced by Brentano's reintroduction of the scholastic concept of *intentionality*—the "ofness" or "aboutness" of every mental state—into modern thought.[10] In *Psychology from an Empirical Standpoint* (1874), Brentano was clearly on to something groundbreaking as he tried to describe how our mental states, such as beliefs and perceptions, get hold of mind-independent facts; however, he was never able to break completely free from the subjectivistic thinking that had led to the skeptical spirit of his age. Brentano would spend much of his life trying to clarify what he really meant, but it would be his best student, Husserl, who put it all together.

Husserl was a Jewish mathematician who, under the influence of Gustav Albrecht, converted to Christianity as a graduate student, and then changed his name to Edmund Gustav Albrecht Husserl. As a mathematician, he was increasingly motivated by wondering how the subjectivity of the knowing process and the objectivity of the objects known could come together in the paradigm of epistemic achievement: mathematical and logical knowledge.

Curiously, Dallas Willard's awareness of Husserl was passed down through another mathematician, Gustav Bergmann (1906–1987). Bergmann had been a graduate student with and close friend of Kurt Gödel at the University of Vienna, Albert Einstein's personal mathematician (because he was a better mathematician than Einstein!) and the youngest member of the Vienna Circle. Being Jewish and seeing the Nazi threat descending over Europe like a coming plague, Bergmann fled to America. Einstein wrote a letter of introduction for him to the University of Iowa because he had heard that they were looking for a professor of psychology and philosophy. For the next forty years, Bergmann tirelessly worked there on the problem of what the mind must be like to account for knowledge.

In 1946 and 1947, William Hay was a young visiting professor at the University of Iowa. There he met Bergmann, who introduced him to the revolutionary views concerning intentionality and the possibility of knowledge that he had discovered on his own and had confirmed by reading Husserl. The following year Bill Hay won a tenure track position at the University of Wisconsin at Madison. A few years later, Dallas transferred to the University of Wisconsin. It was here that things really came together for Dallas. Clearly Bergmann had influenced Hay, because one day, after a few years of study, Professor Hay said to his young graduate student, "Dallas, you are asking all the right questions. I think that you are now ready to read Husserl's *Logical Investigations.*" This would set the direction for all of Dallas's subsequent work in philosophy and religion. Bill Hay died in 1997, and in the memorial booklet for Hay's funeral, Dallas wrote, "Whatever success I have, I owe to Bill's influence. He steadied me and communicated to me that I could do it. Bill had a personal quality of gracious intelligence."

Although Husserl discovered that our psychological processes parallel mathematical truths, he realized that those correlations require explanation. For example, when you think of the Pythagorean theorem, you are thinking of the very same, mind-independent fact that Plato thought of 2,500 years before. Similarly, when you look up into the night sky at the moon, you are seeing the same mind-independent astronomical object that Plato saw 2,500 years before. How is this possible? If mathematical and logical facts are mind-independent, and therefore not in any way made up by us, then whenever we have such knowledge, we have as clear a demonstration as possible that the mind has the capacity to grasp things that are not a part or property of itself. Denial of such knowledge undermines the very possibility of doing philosophy at all. If logic is not objectively true, then why should it have any authority?[11] But clearly, even to raise such a question already requires knowledge of the objectivity of logic. To have such knowledge means that we must already be outside our private "circle of ideas."[12]

The crowning work of Husserl's life was his *Logical Investigations* (1900–1901). In this thousand-page study on the nature of consciousness and its connection to the objects it grasps, Husserl takes on some of the most difficult and disputed problems in philosophy. His momentous conclusion was that almost all philosophers had been thinking of mental states, such as states of thinking or perceiving, in the wrong way. Rather than being mere objects that somehow sit in our minds like apples sit in a bucket, Husserl's great insight is that mental states are *necessarily vectorial*; that is, they necessarily are of something other than themselves. In the words of William of Ockham, mental states are "natural signs,"[13] because unlike conventional signs such as language, one doesn't need access to anything else to know what they are about. They are absolutely unique; there is nothing else in the whole universe that by its very nature points to something else. Each mental state has a subjective or private side, but each also has an objective side, through which it takes the thinker beyond himself or herself to something that is not that mental state. Again, this referential or pointing feature of all mental states is called *intentionality*. Every mental state has this "ofness" or "aboutness," because every mental state *must* be of, or about, something. It is impossible to think of nothing; even if you are thinking of an empty black expanse, that is the object you are thinking of.

This subtle point might not seem profound, but the very possibility of knowledge completely depends on one being able to "reach out" cognitively and "get hold of" objective states of affairs that are outside of one's mind. The nature of the mind is that it is primarily outward directed, as it cognitively grasps mind-independent (public) objects. Unlike so many philosophers from almost every school of thought, Husserl held that our thoughts and experiences are not the objects that we normally examine; rather, they are the things that open up the big, booming, buzzing world for us to explore and understand. In his *Metaphysics*, Aristotle wrote, "For as the eyes of bats are to the blaze of day, so is the reason in our soul to the things which are by nature most evident of all."[14] Nothing is more evident than what our thoughts and perceptions are of, yet this intimate fact (and its significance) eludes most people.

WHAT WE SEE VERSUS WHAT THERE IS TO BE SEEN

Although this chapter is an introduction to the epistemological grounding of Willard's thought, I would be amiss to leave out a final, salient point.[15] Dallas thought that what one grasps of reality—through senses and thought—has as much to do with one's subjective posture toward reality as it does with what is objectively there to be perceived and thought about. If we do not, by our own volition and humility, "hunger and thirst" after reality, or if we live without a love of the truth—no matter how much it challenges our prior commitments—then the truth will simply pass us by (see Mt 5:6 and 2 Thess 2:10). We will be left with our own dwindling resources, attempting to forge out an increasingly futile existence, living in denial of what we suspect might be true. You see it every day. One can avoid acknowledging reality, but one cannot avoid the consequences of refusing to acknowledge reality. Everything in Dallas Willard's academic and personal life pointed toward (he would be the first to insist, far from perfectly) the active presence of God in the world. He thought that every single point of reality was shot through with unfathomable order and wonder, patiently waiting to be discovered.

The possibility of knowledge is relevant to Dallas's account of the spiritual life. The point of his books *The Spirit of the Disciplines*, *The Divine Conspiracy* and *Renovation of the Heart* is that we must adopt specific practices in order to deepen our apprehension of God's activity in the world. If we fail to sharpen our perception of the great spiritual truths as revealed in the life of Christ, God's kingdom, in all its life-transforming richness and power, will simply pass us by. Again, you see it happen every day.

Consider how Dallas's view of knowledge is revealed in his account of the spiritual disciplines, which by design change us so we can see God's presence in the world in an increasingly powerful way. Solitude and silence teach us how to hear God's "still, quiet voice." "What if there turns out to be very little between just us and God?" Fasting teaches us to not have our lives revolve around pleasurable experiences, while studying God's Word allows us to experience the fact that we have food to eat that the world does not know (see Jn 4:32). Secrecy reminds us that ultimately we live our lives before and for God alone. Chastity trains our eyes and minds by reminding us that each person has hopes, dreams, a future and a soul. Worship teaches us that we are not alone in this life, just as prayer teaches us that we do not live only with other needy humans. It forms the habit of confidently including God in every conscious moment of our lives. Confession humbles us by reminding us that we are most profoundly changed by forgiveness and grace. One of the most powerful things I ever heard Dallas say was, "If you confess to a friend that you lied to him, your confession will marvelously enhance your ability to get it straight the next time." How easily and incrementally, even imperceptibly, God's presence in this world becomes dim and distant to us!

The spiritual disciplines help us see God's presence ("the divine conspiracy") that moves through the visible world, but he never forces himself or his ways on us. When avoided or neglected, his presence can easily, and even imperceptibly, become dim, distant and foreign to us. As it turns out, the life spent futilely moving back and forth on the corner of the checkerboard is not limited to the academic world. You can see it every day and everywhere. The whole point of Dallas's work and life was to show us the reality and wonder of living in God's great kingdom now. This is eternal living.

IT'S ALL THERE, WAITING

The life of Dallas Willard, which I was honored to participate in for several decades, reminds me of what Edwin Markham wrote about the death of Abraham Lincoln: his passing from the human scene was like the falling of a great tree—it left an immense and lonesome place against the sky. For those of us who knew and loved Dallas, studied under him or labored with him, ten lifetimes with him would not have been enough. The experience of missing a loved one is a small clue that we were made for eternity. Dallas would be the first to insist that the overarching point of his life was not his presence, but rather, like the intentionality of thoughts itself, the grand and beautiful realities he was pointing to. It's all there, if we have eyes to see, ears to hear, minds to think and hearts to feel. The rest is the adventure of our lives.

Greg Jesson currently teaches philosophy at Luther College and received his PhD in philosophy from the University of Iowa. However, he believes that the heart of his education comes from the twenty years he studied under and labored with Dallas Willard.

From Secular Philosophy to Faith

Brandon Paradise

Nearly fifteen years ago I took three courses with Dallas Willard as an undergraduate philosophy major at the University of Southern California, where Dallas taught for forty-seven years. After going on to law school at Yale, practicing law for several years, and then joining the legal academy as a professor of law I have no doubt that Dallas has had more impact on who I am today than any other person I've encountered. Ultimately he renewed my faith in Christ and his kingdom and thereby radically changed the direction of my life.

So it may be surprising to some that Dallas never evangelized me in any commonly understood sense; that is, during my time as a student Dallas never mentioned the Bible or Jesus or Christianity in any of our discussions. But fortunately for me, I nevertheless happened to stumble upon his book *The Divine Conspiracy*. When I read it in light of Dallas's personal character (which I had observed over the course of three semesters and numerous office visits), it was clear that Dallas personally exemplified the reality of the kingdom that *The Divine Conspiracy* portrays so beautifully.

Dallas's life provided a powerful and compelling evidence of the kingdom life that he describes in *The Divine Conspiracy*. However, his "secular" instruction about the nature of knowledge also played a critical role in opening my mind to the reality of that kingdom and laid a critical foundation for my ability to hear the gospel. So Dallas, by both the way he lived his life and the content of his teaching, imparted to me that a life dedicated to intentional spiritual formation into the character of Christ enables Christ's followers to bring the kingdom into any place that they go—even settings like the secular university where Dallas taught for nearly five decades. Dallas didn't have to mention the Bible to introduce the kingdom. It was his life and logic that won me over.

A Secular Philosophy Course Prepared the Way for Faith

While each of the three courses that I took with Dallas had a tremendous impact on forming my outlook on the world, it was his course on "Twentieth Century European Philosophy" that was most critical.[1] When I enrolled in this course, I implicitly held a naturalistic worldview—"the idea that truth, and reality, is marked out by the boundaries of the concretely existing sciences, and their future"—and would not have seriously entertained the possibility that the Christian tradition constitutes a body of *knowledge* about how to live in the world.[2] However, by the time Dallas completed a series of rigorous lectures on Edmund Husserl, the philosopher on whom Dallas wrote his dissertation, I was convinced that naturalism could not explain how we have knowledge about anything, including knowledge about the natural world.

In his lectures, Dallas presented a detailed overview of Husserl's phenomenological argument demonstrating that naturalism cannot explain how scientific knowledge is achieved. To articulate the point as well as I am able: all scientific hypotheses depend on subjective insight. As a result, the scientific method and all scientific knowledge depend on an a priori, pre-scientific form of knowledge, which is basically intuitional. Husserl therefore demonstrated that the limits of human knowledge could not logically be "marked out by the boundaries of the concretely existing sciences, and their future."[3]

Dallas's lectures on Husserl's arguments against naturalism radically changed my outlook on the world. But there was more. In his lectures, Dallas carefully walked the class through Husserl's view of how human beings come to possess knowledge about anything. While I cannot hope to recapture the intricacies of his lectures, the point that most affected me was Husserl's conclusion that a single method is incapable of producing knowledge about all domains of inquiry. To put this concretely, while the scientific method is well suited to achieving knowledge about the physical world, it is not able to secure knowledge about nonphysical aspects of reality.

According to Husserl, the appropriate method for achieving knowledge about any area of inquiry depends on our experience with that area. This means that knowledge (as Dallas so often said) is "the capacity to represent things as they are, on an appropriate basis of thought and experience."[4] Because what constitutes an "appropriate basis" depends on the subject matter, thought about and experience with a given subject matter is necessary to determine the methods appropriate for gaining knowledge about it. While Husserl offers technical arguments for his claim that we are capable of determining the method suitable to any category of inquiry, suffice it to say that human consciousness works in such a fashion that we can determine what an appropriate basis is and then develop knowledge along that basis.

While I was fully convinced that Husserl had defeated naturalism and had provided the most compelling explanation of the nature of knowledge in general, I did not see (and never talked with Dallas about) the implications of Husserl's view of knowledge for Christianity in particular or religion in general. But I would eventually see the implications.

In the beginning of my junior year in college, I noticed on a friend's bookshelf a copy of a book by a Dallas Willard, titled *The Divine Conspiracy: Rediscovering Our Hidden Life in God*. Curious, I immediately picked up the book to confirm whether this was in fact the same Dallas Willard who was my professor. The back cover author photo proved this was indeed the same Professor Willard I held in the highest regard as the most widely knowledgeable person I had ever encountered. To my amazement, his book was about Christianity—a subject I had never discussed with him and that I thought would be far afield from any interest he would have as quite possibly one of the most learned people in the world. Noticing my curiosity, my friend immediately offered to lend me her copy.

Borrowed during a very busy semester, that copy ended up on my bookshelf where it would sit unopened for nearly two years. Thankfully, at some point after graduation I picked up Dallas's *The Divine Conspiracy*. What I read there gelled together with everything that Dallas taught me about the nature of knowledge and experience. For example, in a statement fully supported by Husserl's claim that the appropriate method for investigating any domain of knowledge depends on the nature of the subject matter, Dallas writes:

> Prayer, it is rightly said, is the method of genuine theological research, the method of understanding what and who God is. God is spirit and exists at the level of reality where the human heart, or spirit, *also* exists, serving as the foundation and source of our visible life. It is there that the individual meets with God "in spirit and in truth."[5]

In other words, *The Divine Conspiracy*'s description of God and his kingdom can be verified by the means appropriate to the subject matter: prayer. While I had been raised as a Christian and was fairly familiar with Scripture, no one I knew had ever talked about prayer as a method of research. But in light of Husserl's claim that the method appropriate to a particular category of knowledge depends on the nature of that category, Dallas's claim that prayer is the appropriate method to gain knowledge of God struck me as intuitively plausible. I wondered, had I missed something important about Christianity?

Even more startling than Dallas's claim about prayer was his claim that eternal life begins now through discipleship to Jesus Christ—a process that entails *learning* how to live our lives as Christ would if he were us. This vision of discipleship was radically different from the conversion model of Christianity in which I had been raised, which emphasizes accepting Christ as Lord and Savior and teaches that eternal life begins after physical death.

The idea that eternal life begins with discipleship to Christ was for me a world-altering revelation. To put it bluntly, early in high school I had become disenchanted with Christianity. This was in large part because Christians did not appear to be any different from anyone else, and, as far as I could tell, were sometimes even less like Jesus than many people who explicitly rejected Christianity. However, after reading *The Divine Conspiracy*'s claim that becoming like Christ involves an ongoing process that includes learning how we can actually come to live in accordance with God's will, it was no longer feasible for me to conclude that Christians were unable to become Christlike. Given my familiarity with American churches, I knew that the vast majority of Christians had neither been taught nor taken up the kind of discipleship that *The Divine Conspiracy* describes.

But I also knew something else: looking back over the course of two years and three classes, I saw that Dallas had manifested in his character the fruits of the kind of discipleship that *The Divine Conspiracy* describes so powerfully. I could not ignore the possibility that not only was Dallas describing the gospel that Jesus actually preached (which emphasizes that eternal life begins now) as opposed to the gospel prevalent in many churches (which emphasizes that belief in Christ is necessary to avoid the wrong side of the afterlife and to receive admission to paradise), but that Christ's claim is actually true: an existentially different quality of life—what Dallas calls "life from above" or eternal life—begins now.

THE KINGDOM IN ALL THINGS

Following my graduation from USC, I enrolled in law school at Yale. After several years in practice, I joined the faculty of Rutgers Law School—Newark, where I teach courses on civil procedure, professional responsibility, race and law, and law and religion. It would be difficult to overstate the impact that Dallas has had on my approach to teaching and scholarship.

Through a life led in and from the kingdom of God, I have discovered that it is possible to bring Jesus' teachings and character to bear on my work as an educator and legal scholar. And learning from Dallas's example, I have found that bringing Christ's character to my work requires that I trust that he can work through me in ways that I do not perceive.

As an educator, Dallas modeled what a follower of Christ is like as a teacher, showing on a daily basis through his gentleness, patience and respect for every student how one filled with the Spirit of Christ conducts a classroom. He also showed me that mentioning the Bible or Jesus is not essential for Christ to work through us, and that manifesting a Christian character is sometimes what is most necessary for someone to hear Christ's message. Indeed, if I had read *The Divine Conspiracy* without ever having known Dallas, I cannot say—given my skepticism—that I would have really heard the message. While I will never know how I would have received it, for me, Dallas's character was confirmation that he was writing from his own experience.

From Dallas's example of reaching me in deed rather than in word, I have learned that to put on the character of Christ means that Christ is always at work in us, whether we explicitly mention him or not. In other words, I trust in him that so long as my character is grounded in his kingdom, he will work through me in ways that I do not perceive.

This kind of trust in God has also had consequences for my work as a scholar, which generally focuses on questions of race and law. Like nearly all areas of legal scholarship and legal discourse, race and law scholarship rarely pays attention to Christ and his teachings. This is true irrespective of the political valence of a particular piece of scholarship. This situation is almost certainly, at least in part, related to the fact that—as Dallas often discussed—a naturalistic worldview reigns in many quarters of the academy, limiting the extent to which the Christian tradition can be perceived to have anything helpful to say on any academic topic, including race and law scholarship.

For me, a daily commitment to Christian spiritual formation has meant a conscious effort to anchor my scholarship (even if implicitly) in normative claims that are likely to be in conformity with a society permeated by the ideal of agape love. It also means that I approach my writing in prayer. From start to finish, I want my work to be rooted in the mind of Christ. After all, as Dallas has reminded us, the early Christians thought of Christ as "master of every domain of life" and every conceivable area of human endeavor or problem.[6] He is therefore the best source of guidance for how the American legal system ought to address racial division and inequality.

TRAINING TO LIVE IN THE KINGDOM

In the years since I first read *The Divine Conspiracy*, I've thought a great deal about its central message that eternal life begins now. But I've probably given even more thought to its claim that eternal living involves our active effort to learn how to live within God's will. As Dallas explains so beautifully in his books *Renovation of the Heart* and *The Spirit of the Disciplines*, learning to live in God's kingdom involves a process of intentional, grace-enabled spiritual formation, whereby a human being is increasingly able to live within God's will and thus to enjoy eternal life now.[7]

As those who have read Dallas's books will know, he provides a sound scriptural basis for the idea that we must train and learn to live within God's will—that it's not automatic. While, as I've described, for me Dallas's personal character played a pivotal role in demonstrating that it really is possible to train to become like Christ and to live eternal life now, years later I discovered that these same ideas have been in the Christian tradition going back to the church fathers. For example, fourth-century church father St. Athanasius the Great taught that through the indwelling of the Holy Spirit human beings are formed in Christ and thereby participate in the divine nature and eternal life, and that the "divinized soul" is one that has achieved a life of virtue through a commitment to Christian spiritual formation into the character of Christ.[8] Likewise, Athanasius's contemporary St. Basil the Great taught that through the imitation of Christ and the grace of the Holy Spirit we are restored to paradise, are given new life and participate in eternal glory.[9]

St. Athanasius and St. Basil are but two examples of a much larger body of early Christians who describe salvation in terms that closely resemble the vision of salvation Dallas sets forth in *The Divine Conspiracy* and elsewhere.[10] In other words, Dallas's claim that salvation is a life and that eternal living begins before physical death has deep roots in the early Christian tradition. Indeed, as I've slowly discovered over years of investigating Orthodox Christianity, throughout the many centuries of its history Eastern Christianity has taught and continues to teach that salvation is a lifelong process of increasing participation through spiritual formation in the divine life of the Trinity.

As Orthodox theologian Stephen Thomas writes in his entry for *The Encyclopedia of Eastern Orthodox Christianity*, Orthodox Christianity holds that "eternal life [is] a state commencing here and now."[11] Moreover, reflecting Orthodoxy's belief that eternal life is attained by *askesis* (spiritual struggle to acquire the indwelling of the Holy Spirit, or in Dallas's terms, Christian spiritual formation), retired Archbishop Lazar Puhalo of the Orthodox Church in America writes, "Saving faith is in itself a moral struggle which begins, is maintained and becomes perfect by God's grace cooperating with man's work of directing his will to the good, towards selfless love by means of sobriety, fasting and prayer."[12]

While a long line of Christians have shared Dallas's understanding that Christian spiritual formation enables human beings to begin eternal living now, many of us who identify as Christians are not aware of this deep-rooted model of salvation. For me, Dallas's personal example of a life dedicated to Christian spiritual formation was the final and most compelling evidence of the truth of what he taught. Because of my own experience, I understand Christian spiritual formation as both a means of enjoying eternal life now and as essential to my ability to share with others the message that we are called to eternal living in the kingdom of God on this side of heaven.

Despite my years of purposeful commitment to spiritual formation, I mostly feel that I remain firmly at the beginning of making the progress that Dallas and many others have made. However, the small growth with which I have been blessed has been a great source of encouragement. In my experience, the hustle and bustle of day-to-day life is one of the chief obstacles to progress in Christian spiritual formation.

In the midst of deadlines, appointments and family commitments it's all too easy to neglect the spiritual disciplines. To help avoid such neglect, I've adopted the practice of fasting on Wednesdays and Fridays and have taken up daily prayers of repentance and Scripture reading. While these practices have led me to ever so slight but nevertheless noticeable progress in putting on the character of Christ, four weeklong retreats that I participated in as a student in the Renovaré Institute for Christian Spiritual Formation powerfully energized my spiritual life. Although before the Institute I had managed to make some degree of progress integrating spiritual disciplines into my daily life, the weeklong retreats were like superchargers, permitting extended focus on the spiritual life in a way that I had not previously done.

While in the culture of the early church it would have been easier for people to believe that it is actually possible to become like Christ, our time and place is much different. Today many people doubt whether the Christian tradition possesses knowledge about how a human being can actually learn to imitate Christ in all things. Indeed, I was such a person when I met Dallas. Thankfully, I was wrong, and I am forever thankful to God's servant Dallas Willard for manifesting the reality of what it is like to live the "with-God life."

In the language of the eleventh-century Byzantine monk St. Symeon the New Theologian, Dallas passed the flame of faith as "from one lamp to another," and thereby helped to form many additional links in what Symeon calls a "golden chain" that connects God's people "from generation to generation" in "one single chain in the one God."[13] For those of us who remain on this side of heaven, by the flame of faith we extend that great chain that has as its end and head Christ our Lord. Through the gift of the Holy Spirit, and through a life dedicated to Christian spiritual formation, let us forever work to the honor and glory of Christ our Lord, who saw fit to give us the life and example of his servant, Dallas Willard.

Brandon Paradise was born in Anaheim, California. He married Soliana Mulugeta of Addis Ababa, Ethiopia, on November 26, 2008. They live in New Jersey.

8

REFLECTIONS ON A DAY WITH MY PROFESSOR AND FRIEND

J. P. Moreland

I loved Dallas Willard. He was like a father to me. I will miss him terribly. Among those who have influenced me most, *he stands out like a giant oak in the midst of saplings*. In Dallas's case, all the things said to eulogize him are actually true. We have lost a five-star general in the armies of God, and the world is not what it was when he was among us.

Dallas was a man with a deep, pervasive, penetrating intellect. He was a Christian first and a philosopher second. From him I learned how to do metaphysics and how to think metaphysically. He taught me to make distinctions when I was blurring categories. He was a committed substance dualist (the view that there is an immaterial soul distinct from the body), and never tired of defending the existence of and talking about the flourishing of the (embodied) soul. He taught me in epistemology to be a direct realist (the view that we can directly experience the real world, in spite of our biases; more on this to follow). And no one knew more than Dallas about the history of ethics, especially in the last 150 years.

He will be remembered most for his writings on spiritual formation, but the man was also a first-rate academic philosopher.

His spiritual writings are not only deep in content, but they also have a texture or tone that accurately expresses Dallas's own life. He lived and practiced what he wrote, and there was a Presence in, around and through his presence. I cannot begin to share all the memories I have of him, but I will mention three, one at the beginning of our relationship and two at the end.

In 1983, while I was a doctoral student at USC, an undergraduate philosophy student named Joe came up to me and asked if I was religious. I assured him that I was not, but that I was, indeed, a follower of Jesus of Nazareth. His eyes grew big and he asked me if I thought Jesus could come up to a person. I had no idea what he meant, so like a good philosopher, I pretended I did and replied by asking him a question! Where did he get this idea? I queried. Well, he said, that morning he had been in Dallas's office, Dallas had led him to Christ, and Dallas had told him that when he prayed to Jesus, Jesus would come right up to him and listen. In typical Willardian fashion, Dallas had put a truth in terms no one had ever thought of, and the way of speaking had its intended impact on Joe and on me.

The next memory is a phone conversation with Dallas three days before he passed on. He was lucid, in good spirits, but so weak that he could hardly project his voice over the phone. He knew he was dying. I told him that I wanted to take a minute to celebrate his life and remind him of the impact for the kingdom he had had. Well, being the humble, unassuming person he was, Dallas would have none of this. I told him he had to listen to me whether he wanted to or not, and he responded that he would take the praise as from the Lord, and I filled his ear with his wonderful legacy. He closed our conversation by remarking on "what a glorious future we all have in the kingdom," and that was how the man approached his death.

Perhaps more important for present purposes is a conversation I had with Dallas a few months before his departure. Through his wife, Jane, he had asked me to meet him at his home for what he knew might be some final words of encouragement and advice. As I was with Dallas that day, I took detailed notes on what he shared. Some of it was personal, but during our conversation he also expressed four concerns he had for the future health of Christianity in general and the spiritual formation movement in particular.

THE NATURE AND IMPORTANCE OF KNOWLEDGE

Before I share these concerns, I should set a context that informs Dallas's words to me. As Dallas once noted:

> The crushing weight of the secular outlook . . . permeates or pressures every thought we have today. Sometimes it even forces those who self-identify as Christian teachers to set aside Jesus' plain statements about the reality and total relevance of the kingdom of God and replace them with philosophical speculations whose only recommendation is their consistency with a "modern" [i.e., contemporary] mind-set.
>
> The powerful though vague and unsubstantiated presumption is that *something has been found out* that renders a spiritual understanding of reality in the manner of Jesus simply foolish to those who are "in the know."[1]

This phenomenon concerned Dallas because he rightly saw that it is on the basis of knowledge—not mere truth or faith—that people are given responsibility to lead and act and live with confidence. The possession of knowledge, especially spiritual knowledge, is essential to human life and flourishing. Thus it is crucial to approach discipleship to Jesus as part of a knowledge tradition. Unfortunately, under the intellectual pressure from contemporary culture many postmodernize (treat as private, subjective, non-rational) the spiritual life, with the result that it becomes just another language game that is hard to take seriously, that does not provide the soul what is needed—knowledge—for a radical commitment to discipleship unto Jesus as the very center of one's life.

Dallas's life and writings provide an alternative to this subjectiv-izing approach: We need to challenge the culture's limitation of knowledge to empirical science and defend an extension of knowledge to include theological affirmations at the core of "mere Christianity." We must insist on the idea that the rich, spiritually formative literature in the history of the church provides knowledge of its subject matter every bit as much as the history of chemistry or other knowledge fields do when they are at their best.

For Dallas, knowledge involves representing reality the way it actually is on an appropriate basis in thought and experience.[2]

Given the magnitude of the role knowledge plays in life and discipleship, it is important to get clear on what knowledge is and is not. Much confusion abounds today about the nature of knowledge, a confusion that hurts people and prevents them from growing in Christ with the sort of confidence that is their birth-right in the Way of Jesus.

There are three kinds of knowledge:

1. *Knowledge by acquaintance.* This happens when we are di-rectly aware of something, such as when I see an apple directly before me, pay attention to my inner feelings or become aware of God. I know these things by acquaintance. One does not need a concept of an apple or knowledge of how to use the word *apple* in English to have knowledge by acquaintance with an apple. A baby can see an apple without having the relevant concept or linguistic skills. Knowledge by acquaintance is sometimes called "simple seeing"—being directly aware of something. In the spiritual life, we can be directly aware of God and his voice.

2. *Propositional knowledge.* This is knowledge that an entire proposition is true. For example, knowledge that "the object there is an apple" requires having a concept of an apple and knowing that the object under consideration satisfies the concept. Propositional knowledge is justified true belief; it is believing something that is

true on the basis of adequate grounds or evidence.

3. *Know-how*. This is the ability to do certain things—for example, to use apples for certain purposes. We may distinguish mere know-how from genuine know-how or skill. The latter is based on knowledge and insight and is characteristic of a skilled practitioner in some field. It can also be called wisdom. Mere know-how is the ability to engage in the correct behavioral movements, say by following the steps in a manual, with little or no knowledge of why one is performing these movements.

Finally, most important is the principle *Knowledge does not require certainty*. Something is certain if it is utterly impossible that one be mistaken about it. In this sense, few things can be known with certainty. Among them are that I exist, that basic principles of math are true (2+2=4), and that the fundamental laws of logic are correct (something cannot be true and false at the same time in the same sense). That's about it. But knowledge does not require certainty, as Paul's remark in Ephesians 5:5 makes clear: "For this you know *with certainty*, that no immoral or impure person or covetous man, who is an idolater, has an inheritance in the kingdom of Christ and God" (NASB, emphasis added). If knowledge is just a sort of certainty, then knowledge "with certainty" would be redundant.

This is no small point. Among other things, it means that one's degree of knowledge can grow or diminish over time. It also means that one can know something and, at the same time, acknowledge that one might be wrong about it. Indeed, the presence of doubt, the awareness of disagreements among experts, or the acknowledgment of arguments and evidence contrary to one's view on something do not necessarily mean that one does not have knowledge of the thing in question. When we seek knowledge of God, specific biblical texts, morality and a host of other things, we should not assume that our search requires reaching a state with no doubt, no plausible counterarguments, no possibility of being mistaken. When people believe that knowledge *requires* certainty, they will not recognize they have knowledge if they lack certainty. In turn, this will lead to a lack of confidence and courage regarding one's ability to count on the things one knows. I am not suggesting that certainty is a bad thing—not for a second. I'm merely noting that it is not required. In the spiritual life, we are after confidence, not certainty.

Central to Dallas's mission in life was the reestablishment of spiritual formation and life unto Jesus as a realm of genuine knowledge in the three senses listed above—knowledge by acquaintance (direct experience), propositional knowledge (true belief based on adequate grounds) and know-how (wisdom, skill). As Dallas often pointed out, we are largely at the mercy of our ideas. Accordingly, his four concerns expressed to me in our conversation that day revolve around promoting this agenda. Two of his concerns were philosophical and two directly involved spiritual formation. Here they are: (1) the explication and defense of robust metaphysical realism, (2) the explication and defense of epistemic realism, (3) the continued development of an intellectually defensible, multidisciplinary model of the human person and of the spiritual life as an expression of human nature and the best path to human flourishing, and (4) the continued development of ways to make the different aspects of spiritual formation publicly testable. Let me develop these concerns in the order just presented.

ROBUST METAPHYSICAL REALISM

By "robust metaphysical realism" I mean two things. First, metaphysical realism is the view that there is a real theory/language/mind–independent world "out there." This is meant to exclude any form of social constructionism, which holds that we as individual or corporate language users construct reality, such as gender, by our acts of theorizing or talking. Dallas would have none of this (he called it "the Midas touch view"). One day in a doctoral seminar I attended during my PhD work at USC, a graduate student claimed that we create the colors of objects so that when we stop looking at them, they have no color. After a few rounds of interaction between Dallas and the student, Dallas put a white cup in the middle of the seminar table, told the student to look away from it, and said the rest of the class would see if it lost its color! Well, when the experiment was performed, the cup stayed white. The student responded that this was because other people were looking at it. So Dallas had each person in the seminar take turns looking away from the cup to see if it lost its color. After one or two did this, the point was made.

As Dallas often said, reality is what you bump up against when your beliefs are false. For him, reality and truth were at the very core of life, especially life in the kingdom.

Second, by "robust" metaphysical realism, Dallas meant that the physical, sense-perceptible world is not all there is. In addition, there is a vast unseen world containing abstract objects (numbers, properties and relations), consciousness and the self, values, laws of logic, God, angels and so on. Regarding the human person, Dallas had little respect for any form of physicalism. For him, it was obvious that the soul was real and that people leave their bodies at physical death.[3] Reductionism and physicalism were false, destructive belief systems in Dallas's way of thinking.

EPISTEMIC REALISM

If anything was central to the entire scope of Dallas's philosophical career, it was epistemic realism according to which human knowers have direct access to objects of knowledge—such as trees, numbers, God—by way of knowledge by acquaintance.[4] This stands in stark contrast to the postmodern view that everything is interpretation.

Postmodernists often reject the notion that rationality is objective on the grounds that no one approaches life in a totally objective way without bias. Thus, objectivity is impossible, and observations, beliefs and entire narratives are theory laden. There is no neutral standpoint from which to approach the world. Therefore observations, beliefs and so forth are perspectival constructions that reflect the viewpoint implicit in one's own web of beliefs. For example, the late Stanley Grenz claimed that postmodernism rejects the alleged modernist view of reason, which "entails a claim to dispassionate knowledge, a person's ability to view reality not as a conditioned participant but as an unconditioned observer—to peer at the world from a vantage point outside the flux of history."[5]

Dallas had little patience for postmodern thought, at least as it is expressed philosophically, and he once told me that it is not consistent with historic Christianity. One of the main reasons epistemic realism was so important to Dallas was that experiences of truth itself are so crucial to the life of the disciple. And that life requires being able to be directly aware of God and his voice, an awareness that is prior to our interpretation of it.

It is beyond the scope of this chapter to engage in a discussion of epistemic realism versus postmodernism.[6] Suffice it to say that, for Dallas, the spiritual life needed to be understood as having a foundation in knowledge, and epistemic realism was the best way to undergird that foundation. For example, if you know a car is reliable, then you will regularly use it and do so with rest and confidence. The same thing is true of centering prayer, fasting and other ways of experiencing God.

DEVELOPING MODELS OF THE HUMAN PERSON AND SPIRITUAL LIFE

For over sixty-five years, *the* central battleground issue in Western culture, especially in the universities, has been the debate about the nature and identity of a human person. Great confusion abounds in this area. As Dallas pointed out, when one is confused about a matter, say, what to do in a situation, then one is not responsible for that matter.[7] How could you be, since no one knows the correct thing to do? Similarly, confusion about the nature of the human person funds ambiguity about how we are and are not to live, which in turn gives people license to be guided in life by sensuality and the immediate gratification of desire.

In this situation, what is needed is a clear, rational depiction of the human person. Two of Dallas's works—*The Spirit of the Disciplines* and *Renovation of the Heart*—represent his attempts to meet this need. This depiction should be consistent with biblical teaching, but it must be supported by rational discoveries from various disciplines, including psychology and philosophy. In developing such a depiction, scientism, reductionism and physicalism must not only be avoided, but also soundly exposed as the irrational, truncated views that they actually are. When an intellectually sound model of human persons is available, the nature of the good life and its relationship to spiritual formation can be located within a framework of publicly accessible knowledge—rather than being promoted as part of a faith tradition for people who need to be comforted by private beliefs.

In spite of the current academic bias against the reality of invisible things, to be accurate and fair to all the data any such model must include the invisible or spiritual. Here are two examples of such items. First, there are a number of eyewitness accounts, some of which have been shared with me personally by credible people, that in alleged cases of demon possession the demon says things about people in the room—specific items of information such as secret sins, childhood events and so forth—that the demonized person simply could not know. These cases should be taken seriously.[8] Second, philosophers are increasingly acknowledging that consciousness—experiences, thoughts, beliefs, desires, volitional acts of free will—is not physical (even if consciousness is deeply unified with the brain) and cannot be perceived by the senses.[9]

Publicly Testable Spiritual Formation

There are two reasons Dallas believed it was crucial to develop ways of testing different aspects of spiritual formation. The first one should be obvious: If spiritual formative practices can be tested for their tendency to produce human flourishing, and if those practices pass the tests, then this would enhance those practices as items of publicly testable wisdom and knowledge. In this way, spiritual formation and the claims made on its behalf could be established as a set of truth and knowledge claims on par with, say, those in the discipline of psychology. Among other things, such a situation would prevent spiritual formation from being privatized and marginalized from the public square.

There is, however, a second reason Dallas thought such testing was important. Dallas regularly insisted that we make experimentation central to our own spiritual journeys. By this he meant that we should try a number of practices until we find those that work best for us. If praying the Jesus prayer a thousand times a day is fruitful, then do that. If using breathing relaxation exercises enhances your prayer life, then experiment with that. In short, experiment, experiment, experiment! Now, one of the important things about such experiments is their ability to be tested against one's own progress in Christlikeness. In this way, testability becomes an important aspect of staying on course in our hot pursuit of Jesus. And Dallas saw this clearly.

WHY A PHILOSOPHER?

Reflecting on these four concerns Dallas expressed for the Christian formation movement, the question comes to mind: Exactly why did Dallas become a philosopher? After all, as a young man he was on fire for Jesus and his kingdom and there were many different career paths available to him for expressing his passion. The answer is clear: Dallas did not govern his life on the basis of truth alone; no, he was centered on *knowing* the truth. And he believed philosophy would help him in that quest for knowledge.

I happen to agree with him, but that is neither here nor there. What is important to note is that for those of us who treasure the man and his work, and who very much desire to stand in, enhance and develop his legacy, we must similarly be committed to knowledge. It is not adequate if we merely promote Dallas's spiritual teachings and allow the culture to continue its depiction of spirituality as a privatized, personal "religious" quest for people who need that sort of thing. We must also do the hard work of grounding this quest in knowledge. I hope you will join me in engaging in that work.

J. P. Moreland is distinguished professor of philosophy at Talbot School of Theology, Biola University in La Mirada, California. He has authored, edited or contributed to ninety-five books, including *Does God Exist?* (Prometheus), *Universals* (McGill-Queen's), *Consciousness and the Existence of God* (Routledge) and *The Blackwell Companion to Natural Theology* (Blackwell). He has also published over eighty-five articles in journals such as *Philosophy and Phenomenological Research, American Philosophical Quarterly, Australasian Journal of Philosophy, Meta-Philosophy, Philosophia Christi, Religious Studies* and *Faith and Philosophy*.

9

Five Tips for a Teacher

Gary Black Jr.

It feels impossible for me to either order or prioritize all the wisdom, insight and effect Dallas and his works have made on my life. Someone recently asked if Dallas was like a second father to me. My quick response was no. That job was taken a long time ago and there has never been a need for another parent. Dallas was my teacher, elder and friend. My father and mother did the rest.

Still, as a mentor and guide into crucial and wonderful realities of our world, Dallas has opened my eyes to the things of God in ways that have deeply formed me. Thus, the opportunity to choose which of these lessons to bring forth in this piece presents me with a great blessing. The blessing comes in the heightened awareness and thankfulness that has flooded over my soul every time I've stopped to consider the wealth of goodness I was introduced to and experienced as a result of our relationship. There are so many wonderful memories, times of life-changing guidance, loving rebukes, encouraging prompts, creative imaginings, belly-busting guffaws and mind-blowing epiphanies (and conundrums) that are forever etched into my mind and soul. The difficulty is choosing among these experiences, for I have yet to find the means by which to sort them all out. Still, I am most grateful for the opportunity to at least try to bless others in the process.

I have settled on a single, meandering conversation we had in 2011 just after I had finished the first draft of my dissertation on Dallas's work. We met at Mater Dolorosa retreat center, where he was teaching a doctor of ministry class for Fuller Theological Seminary. I had enrolled in the two-week class the previous year, and in the months since had unpacked, analyzed and organized nearly one hundred hours of Dallas's lectures in order to integrate them into a host of his previous works and presentations. We met to discuss my analysis and organization of nearly fifty years of his work. Over two days, and a couple of meals, we meticulously went through every theological and philosophical subject we felt was either crucial or interesting for my understanding and analysis of his work.

I can only imagine that for many such an activity would be similar to having an outsider pick through one's intimate and precious collections and valuable treasures, but Dallas seemed to relish every moment. The deeper the conversations went, the more energy he found. Dallas had an amazing love and energy for teaching students, both through his lectures and in more intimate sessions he liked to call "ministry times." In all the many hours I spent with Dallas, even those toward the end of his life when his illness began to sap his energy, I can only recall a very few occurrences when he would end our conversations. He loved to think, talk and process ideas with others.

One of Dallas's most striking character traits was his deep humility. I'll never forget his response to reviewing a bibliography I had created of all the materials, both theological and philosophical, written and audio, that I had reviewed for my dissertation. His reaction was precious. He was genuinely amazed, stunned really. He found himself caught in the wonderment of realizing the depth and breadth of his own portfolio. He admitted to having never seen his corpus laid out in such a way. It was as if he were looking at a collection of mental images, a scrapbook of sorts, full of dear old friends he had not seen for quite some time.

As he glanced down the list he chuckled a few times as a memory was jogged regarding a piece he had forgotten about, and he stopped to offer a little anecdote here and there. As his eyes went through the pages he came to one entry in particular and asked me if I had a copy for him to look at. I fumbled through a box of files and handed it to him. A gleam sparkled in his eyes as his mind drifted to the time, the circumstances, the process and inspiration that led to the creation of that work. As he flipped through the pages his emotions began to rise to the surface. When he handed the pages back to me, with emotion choking his words, he said softly, "That's quite something."

As evening approached we headed to a quaint little British-style pub in downtown Sierra Madre for some dinner. We sat outside as the evening sun softly cast shadows across the sidewalk shops, and our conversation began to shift toward the more personal matters of family, parenting, marriage and ministry. We also began to discuss my hope of teaching in a university or seminary. I was in the process of changing careers and Dallas knew I could benefit from his nearly fifty years in higher education. As was my habit, I had a small notebook with me and began to jot down some notes. When I returned to the monastery that evening, I wrote my reflections on his wisdom. What follows is a significant part of his encouragement and insights.

The Role of a Teacher

What many people familiar with Dallas's more popular works often fail to recognize is the fact that he was a world-class scholar. Further, his devotion to scholarly engagement was a means—though certainly not the only means—through which he was able to gain great depth of insight and clarity on such a vast array of crucial topics that became more widely accepted and recognized by the general public. Yet it was his ability as a scholar to coalesce and clarify matters of ultimate concern that produced the transformative insights his popular readers hungered for and enjoyed.

That evening Dallas wanted to make sure that I too understood what my role and responsibility were as both a scholar and teacher in the making. He believed a teacher's responsibility was to help others come to experience, understand, identify and then accurately represent the realities to which they were devoting their attention. The fact that I was devoting my scholarly endeavors to Willard's own insights and perspectives meant that I too had a responsibility to make sure others accurately understood what he understood as I taught his ideas and insights. He made it clear that such an objective was exactly the same as the goal of the processes of mentoring and discipleship that Jesus demonstrated to his first-century students.

The crucial point was that Jesus, as a teacher, was in possession of knowledge his students did not yet posses, and therefore Jesus' knowledge gave him authority. Further, his students, to be students, must at some point have recognized and appreciated their need for knowledge and discerned the credible sources through which that knowledge void was to be filled. Therefore, Dallas believed there was a mutually dependent relationship required between student and teacher. But he lamented the fact that this is too often not the type of relationship that tends to fill our institutions of higher learning today.

Dallas believed teachers must be able to demonstrate possession of the knowledge they claim to represent, and students must appreciate that fact; otherwise learning, or knowledge transfer and acquisition, is greatly impeded if not impossible. Therefore the teacher's first responsibility is to do everything in his power to assure he is in fact manifesting evidence of the knowledge he claims to possess.

This is something Dallas understood to be an increasingly delicate negotiation between students and teachers at all levels of education, due largely to the degradation of the idea that attaining knowledge or truth was even possible. Further, Dallas understood how aspects of postmodern philosophy had attempted to relegate most knowledge claims to the shadowy arena of abusive elitist power plays. Because Dallas was aware of and empathetic to the tragic abuses of many dubious knowledge claims by increasingly greater numbers of unconvincing claimants, he realized better than most how perilous human existence would become if institutions of higher learning were allowed to substantially eliminate any claims to knowledge and truth.

If the credibility of all knowledge claims became endlessly relative and utterly subjective, one of the consequences would be the extinction of student-teacher relationships, since all knowledge claims and all claimants would soon be deemed equally valid—or equally invalid as the case may be. One of Dallas's most important answers to this impending dilemma was to focus on his responsibilities as a teacher to illuminate the necessity of his role through actually manifesting, or proving, that the knowledge he asserted did in fact exist within his teachings themselves.

As the glow of the streetlights grew brighter, Dallas began to describe what I later realized were five responsibilities of good teaching. He believed the means of accomplishing such a lofty and important role were highlighted in Paul's admonition to Timothy to "pay close attention to yourself and to your teaching" (1 Tim 4:16 NASB). Earlier in the same chapter Paul tells Timothy to exercise, train or discipline himself in godliness (1 Tim 4:7). Dallas's concern and encouragement to me was to focus on the things he believed were potential problems for academics endeavoring to minister the gospel as disciples of Jesus.

FOCUS ON YOUR PURPOSE

The first area of focus or "paying attention" was connected to the issue of purpose. It is very easy in academic work to vacillate and drift back and forth on the ideological winds, not actually deciding on an objective goal for one's scholarly career. Part of the problem with this aimlessness comes from the very intangible nature of academic work. Most academics rarely experience the tangible gratification that exists in most other vocations. Rarely do academics walk away from their endeavors with something concrete such as an architectural plan, the completion of a successful surgery or the foundation laid for a home. Rarely is there a moment when an academic looks back on a month's worth of study and reflection and can state, "there it is."

Even writing, while tangible in terms of letters on paper or screens, has a significant ethereal quality simply due to the indiscernible question of whether it will serve the purpose for which it was created. This is not a problem for most accountants, building contractors, tax attorneys or factory foremen. Dead ends are a natural, and often beneficial, part of the scholar's journey of searching both the knowable and unknowable aspects of one's discipline. Thus, Dallas realized how important focus and dedication are in order to avoid aimlessness, futility and despair.

Of course focus is tied to other aspects of life in the academy as well. Such dedication becomes crucial especially when peers may not approve or appreciate the subjects one is pursuing and why. This can be a significant hurdle since so much of academic life is tied to collegial endorsement, not to mention approval from the consumer/student. As a result, a significant degree of uncertainty and doubt can lead to vacillation about what it is a scholar will endeavor to accomplish. Dallas believed much of "writer's block" was actually caused by fear of taking a position. Fear of others and fear of failure make it very difficult for many academics to settle on an area of study in which they can feel both purpose filled and called to engage.

CULTIVATE PATIENCE

Dallas's second encouragement, to cultivate patience, comes as a continuance of the encouragement to determine a purpose. He was well aware that the results of academic work often do not appear immediately. There are usually long periods of searching, cultivating, mining and then refining information before a discernible and beneficial result emerges. So too, the writing process can be arduous at times. Finding the right combinations of words that clarify yet push into new ideas and explanations that further one's discipline is an art form that takes time and practice to develop. If one does not have a clear purpose and calling in mind, combined with the patience to endure the process of maturing ideas and with the communicative abilities to convey them to others, a scholar will simply not have the stamina and motivation to continue through the developmental years.

ACCEPT SOLITUDE AND SUSTENANCE FROM GOD

Third, Dallas described how lonely academic work can be. This is true not only for the activity of writing—which many writers seem to find is accomplished best in a degree of sustained solitude—but teaching can be isolating as well, especially if students resist or oppose the knowledge being presented. Learning how to be devoted to our colleagues and students in loving and mutually submitting relationships can certainly help. But Dallas believed that each of us must first and foremost learn how to be with God, then with ourselves, before we can be with others in appropriate and helpful ways.

If a degree of solitude is not accepted and properly brought before God, there can be a tendency to artificially acquiesce to peer pressure simply to stem the tide of isolation or to grab at the spotlight of notoriety. Dallas argued that if scholars and teachers were not able to first acquire a secure sense of sustenance and guidance from God, we would find it very difficult to stay the course and do the work we are called to for as long as it takes until the fruits of our labors are forthcoming. Dallas described this sense as an "inner stability" that would enable one to stand alone if required. He knew well that such a quality was just as important in Christian institutions as it was for those employed by secular universities.

The ability to forge one's own course, unaccompanied if necessary, demands a moral courage that is essential for acquiring the credibility for teaching the kind of knowledge worthy of an academic who is a disciple of Jesus. Facing misunderstandings, misjudgments and even condemnation with resolute humility, poise, grace and mercy becomes a primary witnessing ground in academic life. After more than fifty years in the academy, Dallas experienced how the courage to follow one's inner compass is also the primary means through which a faculty member or a faculty can preserve and protect its institutions from falling into the conformity of groupthink.

STAY ENGAGED WITH OTHERS

Fourth, Dallas warned me that in his experience many, perhaps even most, but certainly not all scholars tend to drift into a somewhat distant, often removed, even callous or insensitive relational posture. Sometimes this can be accompanied by less than stellar or underdeveloped social skills. The fact that much scholarly work is isolating and highly intellectual, requiring long periods of deep thought, can also create a habit of living only in the mind, and therefore an imbalance can develop between private introspection and public engagement.

The fact that most of our culture does not live a contemplative life can further isolate the intellectual, even at the intimate levels of familial relationships. Too often our most beloved and crucial relationships with friends and family are marked by a lack of appreciation for what it is that absorbs the scholar's mind and quickens their heart. And the sustained difficulty in sharing the wonder and beauty of these realities can, over time, drive wedges between even the closest of relationships.

As an antidote Dallas recommended the disciplines of service, listening and fellowship as means he used to intentionally draw himself out of the comfortable corridors of his own mind. He encouraged me to routinely practice the intentional discipline of engaging the lives and thoughts of others. He testified how these disciplines, although sometimes awkward for introverts and seemingly frivolous, would, if engaged in a steadfast manner, produce fruits and insights that both enrich and deepen the quality and experience of life and living.

BEWARE OF INTELLECTUAL PRIDE

Finally, Dallas warned me against the dangers and traps of intellectual pride. More specifically, he leaned over the table, looked me square in the eyes, and made a significant point of highlighting the unique and deadly consequences of intellectual pride when combined with religious doctrine. In reference to doctrine, Dallas used to say that if and when one finds they may be accurate in their doctrine, it is only because they are saved. But no one is saved because they proclaim right doctrine. Dallas never believed accuracy was the most important thing in the world; and the tendency of academic life to insist, either overtly or covertly, that accuracy is the final and ultimate determiner of credibility erected a significant stumbling block between truthfulness and authenticity.

Dallas described how our religious institutions and their increasingly acidic polemical disposition have mistakenly equated difference with disqualification and incompetence. The fact that there are over thirty thousand Christian denominations, all professing their doctrinal accuracy, is testament to the value placed on intellectual pride and the priority placed on being "right." In contrast, academics must be careful to maintain a diligent humility in both writing and teaching. Such humility often leads to a degree of tenderness and understanding that will work against the aloofness and insensitivity Dallas previously cautioned against.

Everyday Challenges

As Dallas spoke of the occupational hazards and hurdles of isolation, patience, loneliness, insensitivity and pride, I realized he was speaking to me as one not above these challenges and temptations but as a fellow pilgrim facing these realities every day. We talked about how he encountered these occupational hazards both inside the walls of the church and within his field of philosophy. He recalled how over the years even some of his closest companions remained skeptical and questioning of his ideas and teachings. He talked of periods of deep hurt and rejection, which evoked significant self-doubt and a counting of costs that, in the moment, often appeared too burdensome. I remember him leaning in and grasping my forearm and saying, "But you see, Gary, it's in those times, when the price seems simply too high to pay, it's precisely then when we need to hear and know that we have heard the call from Jesus."

Dallas went on to speak of times of testing, when he was required to seek the grace from God to pay the price and make the sacrifices required of his calling as a teacher. He also spoke of times when he was wrong in his perceptions or conclusions and was required to stop, retreat or quit some activity or project altogether. It was in these pivotal moments that he discovered how crucial it was to hear God's voice. Dallas often lamented that so few people are willing and have made themselves available to the gift of God's guidance. We would often discuss how it was confusing to him why of all his works *In Search of Guidance* (later published as *Hearing God*) seemed to get the least amount of recognition, since it dealt with the most powerful and life changing of topics.

Now, some three years removed from these conversations, I can report that Dallas was prophetic in his words and insights. Each of the temptations he described in such vivid detail has knocked repeatedly on my office door. But what is equally true is that the means of grace and peace he advocated have also given me strength and insight to avoid some, certainly not all, of these pitfalls. As Dallas himself admitted, there may never be a point where aimlessness, isolation, insensitivity and pride are not ever-present potentialities of academic life. Yet knowledge and grace have a tendency to produce and develop a slowly building faith for walking with God in ways that appropriately deal with these issues as they arise. This is something I continue to grow and develop in.

THANKFULNESS

I had the great honor to be with Dallas during his final moments on this earth. I will never forget those last few days we spent together. The final lesson I learned from Dallas while he was alive was to be thankful for my life. Dallas's last words were "Thank you." I can't be sure precisely who or what Dallas was thankful for. He and I were alone in the hospital room at the time, and I don't believe he was thanking me. I believe Dallas was thanking God for his life, all of it, including the radiance of his death.

We would all do well to come to the place where we can honestly thank God for the gift of the life we have, the joy available in living all of our life, right now, in his presence, and the opportunities, gifts and relationships he has provided that make our lives so abundantly blessed and full of purpose.

I miss Dallas terribly. Perhaps I miss him more than any person I've yet lost to eternity. He knew of and lived within God's kingdom reality more than any human being I have yet known. Dallas was able to help countless students, colleagues and friends like myself imagine how their little worlds—whether private or public, religious or secular, spiritual or physical, individual or corporate— could each benefit from the goodness of God and his ways. To no longer have Dallas's wisdom, experience and comforting smile as a readily accessible resource just a few miles away has been a most unwelcome reality.

However, I am slowly coming to realize that Dallas's death has left me depending less on his insights and more completely, more desperately and more thankfully on Christ than ever before. Something I'm sure Dallas takes great joy in. That was always his primary goal for all his students. And that is the final and perhaps greatest lesson I learned from my teacher. Dallas pointed me to Jesus; even in his death, he pointed to the source, never to the servant. This is the final objective of every teaching disciple of the gospel. What a great lesson.

Gary Black Jr. is professor of theology at Azusa Pacific University, author of *The Theology of Dallas Willard* and coauthor of *The Divine Conspiracy Continued.*

WIDENING SPHERES OF INFLUENCE

Dallas's teaching and influence extended far beyond the walls of the university. In this chapter some of his friends and associates from the widespread worlds of business, film, Christian higher education and the church talk about how his vision influenced their work.

Doing Business in the Kingdom

- Eff Martin -

I spent thirty-two years as an investment banker and am now part of a private investing firm. Although I was fortunate to work in highly ethical environments, I found in myself and in many others the natural (but rarely attractive) human tendency toward promoting my own interests and seeking my own gain. For me the root was a deep-seated assessment that my value was based on the three worldly views described by Henri Nouwen: "I am what I achieve; I am what others say about me; and I am what I have."[1] Part of this misconception probably goes all the way back to my childhood, and part of it undoubtedly rubbed off from spending so much time in a business world that exalts power, wealth and influence.

Dallas Willard helped me to understand that I have a different identity as I live and serve in the kingdom of God. I have begun to understand that my value and meaning in life are based on living interactively with Jesus, not on the classic standards of the world. Dallas's familiar teachings that Jesus was the smartest man who ever lived and that we can trust Christ's assertion that the good life consists of living in the kingdom of God made sense to me. Dallas motivated me to want to place my confidence in Jesus Christ and become his student or apprentice in kingdom living.

I first met Dallas at a Renovaré conference hosted by Menlo Park Presbyterian Church. By that time I had already fallen in love with his teachings and had read several of his major books. I took every opportunity I had to hear him teach, culminating in the two-year study program of the Renovaré Institute.

Dallas taught us how we might take on the character of Christ. He taught by both words and example. It is no coincidence that we could say of Dallas what was said of Jesus, "The people were amazed at his teaching, because he taught them as one who had authority" (Mk 1:22 NIV).

Dallas's teaching could be crafted in precise philosophical language, but he could also frame his concepts in a simple popular vernacular. Two of my favorite quotes are, "The world is a perfectly safe place for the Christian" and "God has got your back."[2] During the first Renovaré Institute I formulated my new life view by adopting his language, "I am an eternal spiritual being with an eternal destiny for good. I live and serve in the kingdom of God."[3]

From the beginning of my business career I desired to follow Jesus' instruction in Matthew 6:33, "But strive first for the kingdom of God and his righteousness, and all these things will be given to you as well" (NRSV). Over the years I made some progress in this journey, but failed many times as well. Why did I fail? It usually occurred when I lost sight of who God is and when I failed to trust him. Frequently I slipped back into the view that God demanded I be successful and that it was up to me to make it happen. It was hard for me to realize that God loved me unconditionally and that my value came from knowing and serving him.

When Dallas opened up a clearer picture for me of living inter-actively with Jesus and when I began to believe that "God has got my back," it became much more natural for me to seek the kingdom of God without reservation and as my primary objective. I found that when I began to understand how big and how good God is, I could trust that God, in his infinite love, goodness and power, would be in control of my life and all the people and activities that I cared about.

This mindset revealed itself in many concrete ways. Over time I started to care more about promoting the development and ca-reers of young people than securing further accolades for myself. My stress level dropped when I increasingly realized that the world was "a perfectly safe place" for me because of God's pro-vision. I began to fear less and to see God's hand even in difficult people or business challenges. Today I continue to enjoy the business world and its opportunities, but my greatest joy is in the opportunities I have to learn and teach about spiritual formation and living in the kingdom of God. I am a very long way from being completely transformed, but I am greatly encouraged that the process is underway.

It is interesting to speculate about what would happen if large numbers of leaders in the finance and business worlds focused on Dallas's understanding of life with God. First of all, let me say that I believe many business leaders do in fact function on a very high ethical plane and seek to do what is right as best they can see it. I also firmly believe that financial profits provide the basis for a system that can serve and benefit all segments of society. This will not happen, however, unless the people leading the system act in a particularly enlightened way, a way described by Jesus.

Many of the problems we encounter in our economic system

arise from reasonable activities taken to excess. Greed and un-
bridled ambition sometimes corrupt our business, financial and
political practices in ways that are ultimately extremely destructive.
Perhaps this is because we have not been set free to will the good
of others rather than seeking our own gain. A life lived interactively
with Jesus in which we freely and naturally love by seeking the
good of others would provide a balance and self-imposed restraint
that would eliminate many of the inequities and problems in our
economic and political system.

In this world, our financial markets would be free of abuse and
insider trading. Financial bubbles would occur less frequently and
burst less violently because greed-driven excesses in every corner
would be limited. Companies would be willing to invest for the
longer term and investors would support them. However, less able
executives would still be held accountable for their performance.

Taking a wider view, unions would relax their unreasonable
pension demands while managers would work to balance profits
with fair pay and benefits for their employees. Workplace discrim-
ination and harassment would diminish. Environmental concerns
would become a greater part of corporate cultures, and more companies would take an active role in addressing the social ills of the
communities in which they operate. Changes in the political system
would result in thoughtful economic and social policies that
promote society's greater good rather than serving partisan political interests and protection of political power.

The natural reaction to the foregoing vision is that these ideals
are hopelessly unrealistic. In human terms, I would definitely agree.
However, the question we are considering is about life in the
kingdom of God, where human hearts and behaviors are transformed and leaders begin to take on the character of Christ, where
the will of the individual is being conformed to the will of God. Is
this life even possible? Dallas thought so, and he has convinced me.
In *The Spirit of the Disciplines* his central claim was that "we can . . .

become like Christ by practicing the types of activities he engaged in, by arranging our whole lives around the activities he himself practiced in order to remain constantly at home in the fellowship of his Father."[4]

Dallas's vision of life in the kingdom of God is indeed a radical one. It is the kind of life that led people to say the early Christians were "turning the world upside down" (Acts 17:6 NRSV) and to marvel at how they loved. I believe this style of life would still turn the world upside down—or better yet, right side up.

Eff Martin is a private investor and founding partner of Anthos Capital. He is a former general partner and managing director of Goldman, Sachs & Co. He and his wife, Patty, are deeply engaged in Christian formation ministries with the Renovaré Institute, the Dallas Willard Center for Spiritual Formation, Wellspring and *Conversations* journal. He is also an elder at Menlo Park Presbyterian Church.

Creating in the Kingdom

- *Quinton Peeples* -

"This is important. What you are doing *here*—this is important." Of all the truly powerful things Dallas Willard said in my presence (and there were many), this simple statement hit me hardest. It was at a session he was leading during the Santa Barbara Renovaré cohort. Weakened by cancer, his voice cracking and almost a whisper, he was responding to a compliment, a bit of thanks given for all he had done for us and for the world. But he was also always looking forward, his challenge right out front: He had carried us this far. Now it was up to us. The only question remaining was, would we? Would we be the ones to take his massive amount of insight and clarification, his storehouse of wisdom and grace, and carry it forward to a world so desperately in need?

I believe everyone in the room at that moment said an internal yes. I know I did. But in the days and weeks to come, the challenges to be met required more than acceptance of the mission. The task needed, and still needs, a way forward—a method. I currently know no better way of transforming life than the VIM (vision, intention, means) model Dallas laid out in *Renovation of the Heart*. But how would that method apply to my work, my corner of the world—in Dallas's conception, my "kingdom"?

After twenty years as a writer/director/producer in the entertainment industry, I can tell you that barely a week goes by when someone doesn't ask, "Why are movies/TV so bad?" I rarely give the answer I know to be true: "Because the people making it are bad." Okay, that's hyperbole, but here's my point: the art we create is a reflection of who we are. So if we want something better to watch, we have to become better people.

Now, this idea is radical and won't win me any fans around the office, but since I am speaking from personal experience, I can only talk about what I know. And I know myself. I am a broken, petty, *bad* person, who writes from, and because of, my broken, petty, bad self. Not maliciously bad. Not consciously indulging in my brokenness. But still, my heart with its faults is revealed in what I choose to create. In large and small ways, my worldview makes it onto the page and, if enough people agree with it, onto the screen. If I want the end product to be better, my heart will have to be transformed. If I only go so far as trying to write better stories, this will be a temporary and inconsistent solution. It's simply behavior management (as Dallas has pointed out), and it always fails in the end. Jesus knows this. He always has. That's why he made a point about cleaning the inside of cups.

There will be considerable head shaking and finger wagging from those who would argue that their imagination and professionalism keep their "true" selves separate from their work. Maybe. But to be

honest, I don't see it that way. I've been around the block a couple
of times, and I can tell you that the ideas and images that hold the
most power in Hollywood are reflective of the people who make
the decisions. Someone has to say yes in order for a project to go
forward. And then they have to sign a big check—in our broken
world, there can be no stronger vote of confidence.

What we see on our screens makes it there because a large group
of powerful people agreed that what you are watching is "good," or
at least, "good enough." One need only spend a few minutes with
Breaking Bad or *Honey Boo Boo* to see the prevailing worldview
about quality. And that is a frightening vision indeed.

"*To change governing ideas, whether in the individual or the group,
is one of the most difficult and painful things in human life.*" [5]

In chapter six of *Renovation of the Heart*, "Transforming the
Mind," Dallas lays out a crystal clear articulation of the power contained in ideas and images. For someone like me, who makes a
living creating those two things, the responsibility that comes with
the job cannot be understated. To be truthful, though, I mostly lay
aside any thought along those lines when I sit down to work. I do
this, as most do, in order to "get along" or, if I'm looking for a more
noble rationalization, to "feed my family." Jesus, of course, calls us
to something deeper and truer, but it will take an extraordinary
dose of courage to live into that vision.

But what if? What if I had that courage? First, for anything to
truly change I would have to accept responsibility. Beginning with
myself. But what about next steps? What would it be like if a large
group of creative and business-minded entertainment people took
the wisdom laid out in *Renovation of the Heart* and decided to make
a go of it? What if we took seriously the scholastic maxim of *actio
sequitur esse*—that action is always in accordance with the essence
of the person who acts? Writing, producing and directing would all
be considered actions that reflect my essence. Taking this idea seriously would radically change the kinds of stories I tell and how I

deliver them.

What would our work look like? And, more importantly, what would our *days* look like? Because if we take this idea to its logical conclusion, what we are talking about is holistic—whole life—change. That means the working environment would change, to be reflective of life in the kingdom. A with-God workplace would produce radically different products. Here is where I am not just whistling in the dark. I have been witness to and participated in environments that were Spirit infused, where God's will was at work among creatively minded people. The outcome was extraordinary. I know it can happen. I've been there. But it faded all too quickly, crushed under the burden of the usual banal concerns. It died because, as Dallas stated many times, no one had the vision or intention to continue. It was just a moment and it passed.

Almost immediately I can hear the cries coming from inside myself: *I won't be able to tell the stories I want to tell. Characters will be boring! Isn't this censorship? Shouldn't I be allowed to tell whatever story I want?* The answers to these questions are where the rubber meets the road: The kinds of stories you *want* to tell come from who you are. Check your "wanter," as Dallas would say. Boring characters? It doesn't have to be that way—look at Noah, Moses, Ruth, Samuel, Mary and Jesus. I could go on. And those were all real people. My imagination should be able to kick it up a notch. Censorship? It's not censorship, it's choice. We bring something powerful into the world every time we create something. Is it positive power or negative power? Think about it. And then choose wisely.

Using the VIM model, I can propose something that might look like this: Our Vision is of a landscape filled with entertainment that confirms and explores our human journey under God's care, in all its complexity. Our Intention is to deliver this art using the talents God has blessed us with. And the Means to do so will come from God's provision through people committed to a transformed life and the bounty that comes from it.

Is this too much to ask? I don't think so. Let it begin with me.

Quinton Peeples is a writer/director/producer living in Los Angeles with his wife and two children.

Forming Education in the Kingdom

- Gayle Beebe -

I first met Dallas Willard in an educational setting—in Mudd Hall at USC in 1990. He was the mentor and friend of my mentor and friend, Richard Foster. Richard felt I was long overdue to meet Dallas, and he arranged an appointment at the end of one of Dallas's long teaching days.

Beyond the vivid memories of this first meeting lies the deeper, more profound impact Dallas had on my life and thousands of others. He recognized the great challenges to the Christian life and marshaled his considerable intellect to make not just a reasonable defense for the hope that is within us (1 Pet 3:15), but a compelling portrayal as to why following God, developing a conversational relationship with him, and embodying the life and teachings of Jesus in our own lives is the absolutely best way to live. And he made this case utilizing a variety of tools from his vast intellectual and pastoral arsenal.

Dallas asked probing questions: What is reality? Who is blessed or well off? Who is a truly good person? How do we become truly good people? And how do we know if our answers to those first four questions are even true?

He made provocative statements. Take this one, from the opening paragraph of the introduction to the *Renovaré Study Bible*:

God, in sovereign grace and outrageous love, has given us a

> written revelation of who he is and what his purposes are for
> humanity. . . . This written revelation now resides as a massive
> fact at the heart of human history. There is, simply, no book
> that is remotely close to achieving the significance and in-
> fluence of the Bible. It is truly "the Book."

Who would dare to make such an audacious, category-shattering
pronouncement? Dallas would. He knew what he was asserting. In
the face of the relentless onslaught of secular academic philosophy,
Dallas realized the category of "fact" had a power in the public
square typically reserved for natural science. But he was not only
asserting a fact about religion (normally restricted in the modern
era to the category of human value); he was asserting as fact the
reliability and credibility of the Bible as the source of all that is essential to know about God, his nature and how we gain access to
the best life possible for all humanity: a life with God.

Dallas elevated professional philosophy. He helped us see the
essential importance of philosophy to our own approach to life and
thought. He not only taught philosophy at USC, but he gained a
reputation as an international expert on Edmund Husserl, founder
of phenomenology, the twentieth-century philosophical school
that crafts a philosophical realism based on "intentionality of consciousness." Dallas's impressive corpus reveals a consistent orien-
tation to philosophical realism: that we can know a thing as object
whether or not we know its pure essence, and that what we observe
does in fact communicate or constitute elements of the object's
essence. His approach included a core grounding in intentionality
of consciousness, as he believed that our consciousness as humans
is both shaped by and shapes what we give our attention to.

Dallas radiated personal warmth. Some of my favorite memories
are walking with him during breaks in the *Life with God Bible* project
or during a Renovaré board meeting. Inevitably, after strolling and
talking for a while, he would extend some gesture of warmth and

care that reminded me of Jesus. He expressed empathy and compassion so genuinely and authentically that he always made me feel valued, affirmed and important—and he did it for all of us.

Among the many influences on my life and thought, Dallas alone combined personal care with a brilliant, probing intellect that made the intellectual vigor of Christianity and the attractive expression of God's love so compelling. Richard Foster first introduced me to the majesty of life with God, and his incredible capacity to communicate "experimental, experiential Christianity" provided the leading voice in my own life with God. My thesis adviser at Princeton, Dr. Diogenes Allen, wrote and spoke beautifully of the intellectual credibility of Christianity, but had difficulty communicating the warmth and personal love of God through his own approach to life. For me, Dallas embodied a combination of both men with an unparalleled humility and graciousness.

More than anything else, Dallas embodied the life and teachings of Jesus not to draw attention to himself but to direct our energies to the one and only source of true life. In Greek there are two primary words for life: *zoē* and *bios*. *Bios* is the root of "biology" and speaks to all the attributes that compose our physical existence. *Zoē*, on the other hand, refers to the eternal, uncreated life that originates in God alone. Throughout his biological existence, Dallas repeatedly pointed us to *zoē*.

I find myself today in the same state of mind as countless others: I simply miss Dallas. In different ways, he has touched each one of us. He had that rare and enviable ability to enter the world of whomever he was with. He was so in tune with God that he was able to tune in to others. As the weeks and months pass, I find myself in situations where Dallas previously would have been, and I miss the positive and good effect he had on every circumstance he entered. I miss his ability to lower anxiety. I miss his ability to inspire trust. And I especially miss the way that being with him helped us capture a glimpse of the love of God being carried across the face of the earth.

Dallas was always mindful of his own humanity and that we carry this life in "earthen vessels." But if the Bible is the book that stands as a massive fact at the heart of human history, conveying the nature and purpose of our life with God, then Dallas's life is a massive testimony to the reality and nature of the *only true life*.

As important as Dallas's life and legacy have been, much work remains unfinished, with many initiatives still left for us to carry out. At his memorial service three tributes captured the essence of Dallas's main areas of contribution: the church, spiritual formation and academic philosophy. Dallas reached a wide audience and exerted broad influence with the first two, but we can do much to build on his contribution to academic philosophy. It's too simple to suggest that academics follow Dallas's vision of an educated person. In fact, I can't imagine Dallas considering this the right approach with his colleagues and peers. Instead, he would pose questions that guide each thoughtful person to the proper answers, trusting the Spirit of God to lead and direct the learning process.

To this end, Dallas built a philosophy of knowledge that allowed us both to know everything in its particularity and to see how it fit into a larger, more meaningful whole. He was crafting such a philosophy of knowing when the illness that took his life first weakened his energy and then totally exhausted him. This unfinished intellectual work deserves our interest and concern, and many of his friends hope we will see several great and original contributions as we move deeper into the twenty-first century.

Gayle Beebe is president of Westmont College. His most recent works include *The Shaping of an Effective Leader* (InterVarsity Press, 2011) and *Longing for God*, coauthored with Richard Foster (InterVarsity Press, 2009).

Public Service in the Kingdom

- John Kasich -

I remember the first time I read words written by Dallas Willard. An excerpt from one of his books appeared in a pamphlet, and reading it was like opening a new door into hope and excitement about life's potential. I was compelled to make a number of phone calls to other theologians I respect to check his arguments, and—no surprise to anyone reading this book—they checked out. This was good news because it all sounded too good to me.

Dallas Willard argued that real life and real power is found by connecting to God—experientially, in this life, in real time. In fact, he suggested that our true purpose in this world is to be good stewards of God's kingdom, to work with God's power to help heal this world, and to learn to navigate the ups and downs of life, realizing that they help strengthen our souls for the world yet to come. The New Creation or next life, according to Dallas, will be filled with joy and love and fulfilling work for eternity. I've read and reread *The Divine Conspiracy* and recommended this book to many others. *The Spirit of the Disciplines* has given me a road map on how to establish a real connection to the Lord through silence, reflection, study and prayer. While I often fail to exercise these disciplines because of the fast-paced life we all live (and I realize Dallas would challenge my acceptance of hurry), I am convinced his advice is good. Just imagine that a person can align with the will of a just and loving being and use it for good while shedding selfishness and ego that hold us back from real power.

I wish I could do better; however, we must not dwell on our failures but instead focus on small but real changes that lift us from our most basic nature. Dallas Willard has given me this hope and goal, and he's pointed me to a guideline or game plan for authentic transformation. I have hope that I can put practices in my life today that can help me not only now but also in the world yet to come—

that is, eternity. So when I get knocked down, I'm empowered to get up, and equipped to do better. And I'm not doing life alone!

I had the chance to speak with Dallas Willard on the phone on several occasions. I was struck by the deep tone of his voice. It was a voice of authenticity, patience and kindness. We talked of the New Creation and of our mission today. I felt like a student speaking with the master. I am so grateful to have made this connection, and for Dallas's writings. They've changed my life. And I love to envision the potential impact on society if more and more people in government began to live lives of other-centered love.

John Kasich is the governor of Ohio. He and his wife, Karen, have twin daughters.

Doing Church in the Kingdom

- John Ortberg -

What kind of world is our earth created to be? And what kind of church would such a world need? And what kind of leaders would such a church need? Often those of us in the press of day-to-day ministry in church work are so preoccupied with meetings to run and sermons to write and staff to oversee that we simply lose sight of the larger questions that cry out for thoughtful response.

Much of Dallas's life was given to these questions. His early decision to enter the academy rather than pastoral ministry was partly a reflection on how the church itself needed thoughtful help, as well as the academy. The church, like other institutions Dallas addressed, is governed by ideas, and often the most important ideas are so pervasive that we hardly recognize their existence.

In our day, the governing idea for those of us in church ministry is the default assumption that bigger is better. I remember a conversation with Dallas where he noted that when he and Jane were young, no one ever seemed to ask whether a pastor was "successful." Pastors came and went at churches; everyone knew that some were more suited for their work than others. But there was not the grinding, relentless pressure to compare oneself to other practitioners. There wasn't the same chronic sense of comparison between one church and another. There was not the same level of celebrity culture impacting the life of the church.

So what would the church look like if it were invaded afresh by the reality of the kingdom in our midst?

To begin with, pastors would be happy.

They would be, within limitations of temperament and genetic restrictions, the happiest people in their congregations. This happiness would not be dependent on "how the church is doing" in external or superficial ways. It would be true because the pastor had taken it upon herself to make her first task living in deep contentment, joy and confidence in her daily experience of life with God.

Pastors would do this for the same reason that any sane person would do it: out of recognition that this with-God life really is the pearl of great price that any non–cognitively impaired human being would sacrifice everything to obtain, and would make the sacrifice with joy.

Pastors and church leaders would make living out of this reality their first priority for roughly the same reason that airline passengers are told to put on their own oxygen masks before trying to help the passengers next to them: it is very hard for a dead person to help anybody. If a pastor is going to be helpful, he must start by actually being alive.

If churches were working rightly, they would recognize this dynamic and cheer on their leaders in the quest to realize such a life. They would not do this by giving the pastor lots of time off and lowering the standards of contribution and fruitfulness.

Pastors, like people in other occupations, have contributions to make and accountability to attend to. Pastors cannot call for other people to care for souls during "time off" if we expect to do it only during "time on."

Instead, churches would pay particular attention to the kind of persons pastors are actually becoming. Part of what that means is that there would be a level of honest conversation and authentic conflict that churches (even churches that say they're interested in spiritual formation) often avoid with greater sinfulness than marketplace businesses.

If the kingdom were to break into the church with greater freshness, people would look at pastors and say—in the words of an old movie—"I'll have what she's having."

Out of this rich life would come gifts for the church. One would be a priority on the quality of the actual persons that churches are producing. Too often churches aim at producing people who affirm the right beliefs and avoid the wrong sins, along with certain behavioral compliance related to giving and attending and serving. When the kingdom comes with substance, the texture of actual lives and deeply embedded habits begin to be attended to and noticed and challenged and cleansed.

Then the church can become what Dallas would call a "school of life"—the angels of heaven evidently ascending and descending to bring a new dimension of power to human character.

This would also mean experimentation and growth toward what might be called the Holy Grail of spiritual formation in our day—the discovery of a life-giving way of life through which contemporary people in our society actually receive power from God to change.

The lack of this concrete "way" of Jesus in our day is an enormous barrier to both spiritual transformation and evangelism. The lack of a concrete way is partly responsible for the misunderstanding of the gospel in contemporary evangelicalism.

In Jesus' day, the call to follow him was wonderfully concrete. People knew whether or not they were following. It was a physical act of committing to proximity to his body. After his ascension, such a decision was still very concrete but now it involved proximity to his body the church. Passages such as Acts 2 help us see how radically different this way of life was for those in the ancient world.

By the time of Constantine the power of the Way had been diluted. When a majority of members of the Roman Empire professed the Way, it lacked the distinct practices and edges to connect people to transcendent power. Because of this, those hungriest for spiritual power went into the desert and sought again a way that could speak to their unique day.

The pursuit of a life-giving way runs across the ages. We see it with the emergence of AA. We read of it in Wesley, or in *Life Together* by Bonhoeffer. In the United States, Christianity is so sufficiently diluted that it's not clear that simply "going to church" puts someone in touch with this Way. So the gospel tends to be transmuted into "How do you know that you're in the heaven-bound group?" The main need is not simply a better way to articulate the gospel (though that is needed); it's a concrete expression of the Way of Jesus that can bring transformative spiritual power to people living in our society and conditions and pace and culture.

When the kingdom lands more fully on the church, the church will move toward becoming such an experiential school of life.

And from there, it can move on to its calling to be "teacher of the nations." Currently, we have far too strong a sense of "us versus them." One of the most remarkable dimensions of Jesus' person and ministry and message was his obliteration of in-group versus out-group distinctions. It was as if he thought all persons were—potentially if not already actually—a part of his in-group.

Always the calling of Jesus is immensely larger than the appeal of Christianity or the scope of local churches. This is because to be human means to need to learn how to live. And no one yet has been able to live, or to teach how to live, like the crucified carpenter. When the kingdom is more fully guiding the church, then the great questions of human direction and human transformation can once more receive a fair hearing in our day, as they come from the One who alone gives hope.

So the church would be led by happier people, and produce more loving congregations, and bless a more open world, if the kingdom among us were more fully realized by those of us called to be its leaders, under the watch-care of its Primary Sustainer and Most Glorious Inhabitant.

John Ortberg is senior pastor of Menlo Park Presbyterian Church. His most recent book is *Soul Keeping.*

PART THREE

Mentor and Reformer
of the Church

The Memorial Service

On May 25, 2013, seventeen days after the intimate funeral and burial of Dallas Willard, hundreds of people poured into the auditorium of the Church on the Way in Van Nuys, California. The sanctuary, known as the Living Room, was huge and filled with rows of blue padded chairs. In the center of the stage a modest wooden podium stood in front of a screen used for filming. Purple and orange triangles and tilted squares hung to form a brightly colorful backdrop. A set of drums was tucked away in the corner behind Plexiglas, confirming the charismatic leanings of the congregation. No one played them that day.

The individuals who gathered in the room came from all walks of life—college presidents and college dropouts, business elite and unemployed, successful editors and those who had no desire to write, megachurch pastors and house church attendees. One arrangement of flowers had been sent from the governor of a faraway state, another from an apolitical resident of that same state.

A man raised in obscurity as a child lived a life that changed the lives of tens of thousands. It had taken a four-column-wide article in the *Los Angeles Times* to cover the story of his death. The tribute appeared under the heading "Dallas Willard, Influential Christian Philosopher." Ironically, most of those gathered knew little if anything of Dallas the philosopher—and probably could not spell Husserl. They knew Dallas as a Christian, the type that gave you hope that the promises Jesus made about abundant living could actually be cashed.

Jack Hayford, founder of the church, opened the service. He had come to that location in 1969. Dallas would have been thirty-four at the time, preceding Hayford to the valley by four years. Hayford explained the logic behind holding the service in a church Dallas did not attend. The two had became longtime friends—there is even a video of them singing "Majesty" as a duet—and had often shared the stage at large gatherings of pastors. Dallas and Jane often had listened in from their sofa to broadcasts from the church. Plus, a really big place was needed for this service.

Many of the individuals who followed Hayford to the stage to speak—Becky Heatley, Richard J. Foster, Larissa Heatley, J. P. Moreland and John Ortberg—have essays in this book, so we will let them speak for themselves. For those in the room that day, the tributes created alternating waves of laughter and tears.

Perhaps the ultimate Rorschach test of a person's life is the music he chooses to be played at his memorial service. Dallas chose "Never Alone" for the first song. One could argue that through those words and haunting melody, Dallas had enjoyed the divine promise of being able to live intertwined with God, caught up in a presence from which nothing can separate.

Another song was a hymn that the family found in Dallas's Bible. The title is "May the Mind of Christ, My Savior." The words of the first two verses express volumes about the man who loved it.

May the mind of Christ, my Savior,
Live in me from day to day,
By his love and power controlling
All I do and say.

May the Word of God dwell richly
In my heart from hour to hour,
So that all may see I triumph
Only through His power.

Because of Dallas Willard's teaching about eternal living, it was easy, I believe, for those attending to file out of the sanctuary believing that Dallas's words to his dear friend, Richard Foster, would be true for them as well: "We will see each other again."

MASTER OF *METANOIA*, BERMUDA SHORTS AND WINGTIPS

James Bryan Smith

I first met Dallas Willard in 1983. He spoke at the annual convocation week at Friends University, where I was a student and Richard Foster, who had invited Dallas, was a professor. I listened to every single lecture, bought the cassette tapes of his talks afterward, and listened to them again. I did not understand anything he said, but he sounded really smart, and he seemed genuinely humble. I drove him to the airport, and he was very kind.

Then in 1987 Richard brought together a group of people to be on the board of a ministry he had named Renovaré (Latin: to renew) as a means of bringing a balanced vision and practical strategy for the renewal for the church. Dallas and I were both asked to be on that board, along with other luminaries such as Bill Vaswig, Marti Ensign, Roger Frederickson and Edward England. I was a mere twenty-six years old, working as an assistant pastor in a Methodist church. I was way out of my league, but they were all gracious to me. Dallas in particular always made time to ask me about my life, and to allow me to ask him questions, which I did frequently.

We held our first conference in 1988, and Dallas gave a talk on holiness that blew my mind. Prior to the talk I had thought of holiness as drab and boring and hard. Dallas actually said that in his talk: "Most of us think of holiness as pale and lifeless. Holiness is actually bright and alive. Holiness is wholeness. It is the way life is meant to work." This was the beginning of the countless ways Dallas would cause *metanoia* (a Greek word often translated "repent," but which actually means "change the way you think about . . .") in me.

Dallas, like Jesus, was a master at helping others experience *metanoia*. We all live by framing narratives. They help us make sense of our world. We are told something (for example, "God is full of wrath and anger"), and then we put a frame around it in order to see it and understand the world by it. What Dallas did constantly was challenge my false framing narratives—ones that were secretly causing a lack of faith, hope, love and joy, though I did not know it—by offering me a new framing narrative.

When someone challenges your framing narrative, your first reaction is disbelief. The second reaction is to challenge back. Dallas was a master at challenging your narratives in a gentle yet persuasive way. He never forced his opinion, and he always had an answer to a rebuttal. He simply wore you down with truth, and in the end you were more than grateful to him because, as he often said, "Reality is what you bump into when you are wrong," and it is nice to stop bumping your head.

THE MAJOR FRAMING NARRATIVE SHIFT

I would go on to see Dallas many times and hear him speak at Renovaré events between 1988 and 1994. But in 1995 I was asked to serve as a teaching assistant for Dallas in the summer course he taught for Fuller. The class lasted two weeks, and Dallas lectured for about eight hours a day. This meant I, and the other forty students in the class, would hear him teach for approximately eighty

He Made Me Feel Welcome and Told Me a Joke

Emilie Griffin

I met Dallas in the 1990s when I was first joining the Renovaré speaking team, and I liked him right away. The way it worked out was that Richard Foster, Dallas and I were all speakers at a conference at Forest Home in California.

I found the whole experience to be exotic. The terrain of the American West struck me as biblical. I was Catholic, and Renovaré was an evangelical group, yet it all seemed heaven sent.

Dallas had a tremendous sense of humor—sometimes pretty sly. My favorite recollection is of Dallas telling a joke at the dinner table with a number of people present during a Renovaré conference in Salem, Washington. The joke was about someone who died and went to hell and discovered Martin Luther there. Dallas had a deadpan delivery. "Why, Dr. Luther, what in the world are you doing here?" and Luther answered, "It was works after all."

I didn't know at first if I was allowed to laugh. I wondered if they were testing my theological savvy. Then Dallas sort of twinkled at me. He did that.

Dallas and Richard were checking me out.

I decided the whole group was wonderful and hoped they would ask me to join. Which they did.

My last face-to-face visit with Dallas Willard was at the Renovaré ministry team gathering in June 2012. Even though he was weakened, he gave three days of teaching on the Bible, but we knew he was facing surgery. It was an amazing time. Dallas, Jane and I said a brief goodbye, and I think we used the words "here or hereafter."

As I reflect on my friendship with Dallas I notice how often, how gracefully, he encouraged me. I was eager, full of aspiration, and conscious of the blessing and challenge of high intellect. How was I best to use that in behalf of what I believed, and the Master I longed to serve? Perhaps the most tender moment for me came when I gave

Dallas a copy of my book on mysticism, *Wonderful and Dark Is This Road*. I asked for his evaluation. We were at a small Renovaré meeting in Texas, shortly before a larger conference began. I gave him the book after lunch, expecting he might take it back to California and have a look. He reappeared several hours later at dinnertime and said he had read the book straight through. He wanted to commend it. He wrote the commendation then and there, by hand. Among other things, he said, "She demystifies mysticism, but in a way that does not lose its depth and power."

I treasure his words, not only because mysticism is a vast topic and Dallas thought I had made it accessible. I treasure his words because I wanted so much to know that he and I were somehow together, walking together, joined by our common love of Jesus Christ. Scholars and speakers and even disciples may disagree now and then, but the love of God transcends all that. It heals us and makes us whole. Dallas Willard was a friend to many. And he was a friend to me.

Emilie Griffin is a writer living in Alexandria, Louisiana. Her most recent book is Green Leaves for Later Years *(InterVarsity Press).*

hours during that span. Dallas had been writing the early drafts of what would become *The Divine Conspiracy*, and his lectures were largely based on the content of that book. I was simply not prepared for what was about to happen. I did not deserve the title of teaching assistant, because I could not understand the teaching myself, much less be able to assist anyone else.

That first course was held on the campus of a private Christian school. The people at Fuller arranged for Dallas and me to stay in the home of one of the faculty members who was gone on vacation. The owner of the house was an art teacher, so the home was full of art, though none of it was to my taste. It was gothic, dark and kind of scary. On the refrigerator was a note asking us to watch over their cat during our stay, and it said at the end, "He doesn't stay in the house much, but please put out fresh food and water. You won't be able to miss him. He is white, and has only three legs." I felt disoriented. And it was about to get worse than merely weird art and a three-legged cat.

The first day Dallas asked the class, "What was the gospel, or good news, of Jesus?" The students, most of them pastors, began saying things like, "Jesus came and died for our sins so that we can go to heaven when we die," or something close to that. After a while there was silence, and Dallas said forcefully, "No. That was not Jesus' good news. His good news was about the availability of the kingdom of God." I could see the disbelief on their faces, and if I had had a mirror I would have seen it on mine. Dallas went on that entire morning teaching directly from the Gospels and Acts, walking us through passage after passage, wearing us down with the truth that had been right in front of us all the time, but we had missed it. Every one of us was a seminary graduate, and we had missed the most fundamental aspect of ministry.

I would go on to assist Dallas in that summer course for the next seven years. It took me about three years to grasp what Dallas was saying, and another four to see its implications. But each year I would watch a new crop of students undergo the same *metanoia*, the same narrative reframing, and I began to see a pattern—similar to the Kübler-Ross five stages of grief. For a few days the students were in denial: "This cannot be right." Then on about the fourth day, when the *metanoia* had occurred, they would get angry: "Why did no one tell me this? My pastor never preached this, and my professors never taught me this—how could they?" I never saw much bargaining or depression, but by the end of the two weeks they all had come to acceptance. And subsequently, to a major pivot in the way they lived and in what they taught and preached.

DALLAS UNPLUGGED

During that first class I also got to see, for the first time, what I call "Dallas unplugged." By that I mean seeing the man not in a pulpit or podium, but fixing breakfast or watching television. He wore the same brown wingtip shoes every day, with brown socks. But when he got home he changed out of his trousers and dress shirt and put on a pair of Bermuda shorts and a white T-shirt. But here was the best part: he kept on the brown socks and wingtips. So he looked dressed up from the ankles down. It was an odd look. But then again, we were staying in an odd house with an odd cat, so it all kind of worked. The television we were watching was old and had no remote, so you had to walk to the set to change the channel (the old days).

Watching TV with Dallas was one of my favorite parts of these summers. Since 95 percent of what is on TV is inane and superficial, I was surprised to learn that Dallas liked to watch it at all. He said it helped his brain to slow down. His running commentary was insightful and often very funny. While watching a nature show about alligators, in which the camera kept showing an alligator slowly moving toward a huge frog, Dallas quipped, "That frog is not long for this world." I laughed out loud.

One other evening Dallas got up to change the channel and was flipping through when he stopped on a Spanish channel in which people were doing a salsa dance. Dallas looked at me and said, "Well, that looks fun. I should try those moves." At that instant he began dancing along with the people on the show. The sight of Dallas doing the salsa in a T-shirt, Bermuda shorts and wingtip shoes made me fall off the couch in hysteria. That image is burned into my mind today, and when I recall it I always smile. The smartest man I have ever met had the humility and whimsy to just be silly.

Brilliant but Balanced

Dallas really was, by far, the most intelligent person I have ever known. During the spring of 1998 Dallas and I teamed up to lead five Renovaré conferences, literally from coast to coast, from San Francisco to Washington, DC. When we checked into the hotel in San Francisco, the young woman at the front desk greeted us, and I noticed she had an accent, but I couldn't tell where she was from. So I asked her. She said she was from Hungary. I thought to myself, "I don't know anything about Hungary. I probably couldn't find it on a globe."

As we walked toward our rooms I said, "I don't know anything about Hungary, and I feel kind of stupid." Dallas said, without missing a beat, "Oh, Hungary. Well they have a new leader recently elected, and are going through some difficult financial times, and . . ." He went on to tell me more and more about Hungary, and by the time I reached my room it occurred to me: "How much does this guy know? Is there anything he *doesn't* know?"

But he was not just brilliant, he was balanced. He was normal, and kind, joyful and generous. I spent many hours in airports with Dallas, waiting for planes, often delayed. Dallas always remained calm when everyone else seemed at their wits' end. He would hum a hymn, or pull out his Bible and start memorizing a new passage. I always bombarded him with questions, and he never seemed bothered by them. One time our conference host failed to book separate rooms, so poor Dallas was stuck with me, asking questions the entire time. "So Dallas, which do you think is right, Arminianism or Calvinism?" I hadn't noticed that he had gone into the bathroom to brush his teeth. He poked his head out, with a mouth full of toothpaste, and said, "One moment, please." I apologized, and when he came out of the bathroom he looked at me and said, "Neither." He went on to say that both were right, and both were wrong, and he did not fit into either camp.

His knowledge of the Bible astounded me. He seemed to know its contents from cover to cover. I discovered why in that first class. After a little television watching, Dallas would excuse himself and go to the dining room. I peeked in to see what he was doing, expecting him to be preparing for the next day's lecture. He wasn't. He was studying the Bible. He was taking notes, writing on note cards and working on memorizing whole passages.

His pastoral skills were exceptional. He was a great listener, and very compassionate. I never felt judged by him. Not once. He certainly could have corrected me, but he seemed to take the posture that if I needed correcting the Holy Spirit would find a way to do it. As an academic he was not averse to taking a position or disagreeing with someone, but he did it with dignity. I think he saw his work as a scholar as completely compatible with his work as a pastor. He combined wisdom with love like no other.

When our daughter Madeline was born with severe birth defects due to a chromosomal disorder, we were told by the doctors that she would likely not survive birth and had no chance of living more than two years. I called Dallas and Jane one evening from the hospital, and they began by telling me they had been praying for us. I poured my heart out to them, crying mostly, and they listened and comforted me the entire time. What they shared, they had learned from having walked through their own dark valleys.

I told Dallas I was at a loss about how to pray for her. He asked, "If you were God, what would he want to hear from you?"

"I don't know . . . I suppose he would want to hear what is in my heart. He would want me to tell him what I want, and how I feel."

Dallas said, "Exactly. You must do that."

"If I tell him how I really feel I am not going to be nice."

He said, "God can take it. Haven't you read the Psalms? Just tell him what you want, like a child to its father."

"I want her to be well. I want her to dance one day, to grow up and get married and live a wonderful life."

"Then tell him that."

"But I can't," I said. "I don't have faith that this will happen. Don't you have to have faith when you pray?" I asked.

"It isn't a matter of faith. It is a matter of telling your Father what you want."

"All I can do right now is say to God, 'Thy will be done.'"

"You don't need to tell God that, Jim. He knows you accept his will. He doesn't need a reminder. And quit worrying about your level of faith. Just tell him what you want, and keep telling him over and over. Don't tell him once, tell him every day."

As usual, he reframed my narratives, this time about prayer. He did this all the time, about so many subjects I cannot count them all. He blew up my framing narrative about the gospel, about the church, about life's ultimate meaning and about how we actually grow spiritually.

And he did it with such incredible verbal acuity. He found ways to sum up his counter-narratives in single sentences, such as, "The kingdom of God is never in trouble. And neither are those who are in it"; or "We live at the mercy of our ideas. They run, and often ruin, our lives"; or "There is no problem in the world today that apprenticeship to Jesus cannot solve"; or "The main thing you get out of life is the person you become." His phrases were so good they were impossible to put in other ways without losing something. I would often confess, "Dallas, after all these years learning these life-changing truths from you, I find myself quoting you all of the time. But don't worry, I always credit you." He said, "You must stop doing that, Jim. If it is any good, it did not come from me but from the Holy Spirit. I actually ask the Spirit to give me those phrases. So consider it public domain."

Ongoing Impact

Because of Dallas's impact on me, I see everything through the lenses of the available, present, powerful and provisional kingdom of God. It only took Dallas five years to get me to see that this was Jesus' gospel, and another fifteen years for me to live into it and see and experience its reality. Thanks to Dallas, the master of *metanoia*, and this new, accurate, biblical framing narrative of life in the kingdom, my heart is being changed. Here are some of the ways.

First, I have a governor on my worrier. I still worry, but I don't worry as much and for as long as I used to. Second, my forgiveness time is shorter. I still get angry with people who hurt me, but I forgive sooner and more easily because of Dallas. Third, my default self-centered thinking (I, me, mine) gets overridden more often (we, us, ours). I am still self-centered, but not as deeply and a little less often because of what Dallas taught me. Fourth, I face my disappointments with less frustration and more serenity. I still get disappointed (daily, if I am honest) by people and events and myself, mostly, but the disappointments seem smaller and less obscuring.

All of these changes in my life came from the deep, eternal narratives that Dallas taught me and so many others. He made it clear that the kingdom of God is never in trouble, the kingdom of God never runs out of resources and the kingdom of God is never lacking in power. Therefore, those who live with God in this available kingdom are never in trouble, never lack provision and never lack power. In the kingdom of God I discover that I am safe, significant and strong. I will forever thank God for his servant Dallas Willard, who taught these truths with authority.

Dallas—both his life and his teaching—continues to affect my life on a daily basis. When I think I don't have the resources to accomplish something, I stop and remember that if God is in it and for it, then together we can do it. When people do things that hurt my feelings, I stop and remember that they too are fighting a great battle, that they are my brothers and sisters, that my identity is in Christ and I am secure, and I find the courage to forgive. When I catch myself asking "What's in it for me?" I stop and remember that it's not all about me, it's about a divine conspiracy that involves the well-being of all people, of which I am merely a part. When things do not go as I think they ought to, when I feel sad and disappointed, I stop and remember.

How could one man have had such an impact on me? Because he knew and experienced Jesus' gospel, and became the kind of person who embodied all of these things and more. This way of living is more caught than taught. Dallas certainly taught me a lot, but I caught so much more from just watching him, from watching him and Jane conduct their lives with kingdom dignity, faith, joy and wisdom.

These days I stop and remember Dallas every day. I have a picture in my office of us together. When I look at it I stop and remember what he taught me. I stop and remember how he lived. And I will never stop remembering him until that glorious day when I will not have to remember him anymore because I will see him face to face, shining so brightly that I will strain to see him. I just hope he is wearing a T-shirt, Bermuda shorts and wingtip shoes, and dancing the salsa.

James Bryan Smith is professor of theology and director of The Apprentice Institute at Friends University in Wichita, Kansas. He is the author of *The Good and Beautiful God.*

Journey into Joy

Trevor Hudson

The question began a journey into joy.

Dallas had asked me to comment on *The Divine Conspiracy* as he wrote it. Every few months there would be a newly finished chapter in my mailbox. The explosive themes of the first two chapters—the invitation of Jesus to experience eternal living right now, the integration of our little kingdoms with the big kingdom of God, the limitations of the gospel of sin management—challenged me deeply. But the opening theme of the third chapter did not. It evoked tremendous resistance.

In this chapter, Dallas shares his understanding of God. His starting point for his re-visioning of what God's own life is like took me totally by surprise. Dallas makes the bold claim that God "is the most joyous being in the universe."[1] This unusual phrase stopped me in my tracks. I had never heard God described in this way before. And I simply could not accept it. Indeed, it would be more accurate to say that I strongly rebelled against this notion of a joyful God. There were two reasons for this resistance, I now realize.

On the one hand, I was reading these words against the background of apartheid South Africa. The suffering caused by this unjust system was overwhelming. It was hard to picture God being happy while millions were suffering from oppression. To do so would have seemed to strengthen the already prevalent idea among the oppressed that God didn't really care about their situation. Personally I had become convinced that we needed a theology much more focused on the crucified God who suffers with us.

On the other hand, there was also a more personal reason. I did not rate very high on the joy meter myself. Not only did the senselessness of the suffering around me take me to dark places in my own heart, but my temperament was constantly characterized by dissatisfaction and discontent. Those around me, especially Debbie, my partner in marriage, would frequently share concerns about my pessimistic outlook on life. Joy was definitely a stranger in my life.

But let me return now to that question. I remember the exact moment Dallas asked it. We were sitting together in a parked car outside the home of a friend. As we spoke about the third chapter of his book, I told him about my resistance to a joyous God. Recalling Bonhoeffer's conviction that it is only the suffering God who can help us in our pain, I said, "I miss any reference to the crucified God. Surely God always suffers with us? How then can God be the most joyful being in the universe?" In his own typical way he responded to my questions with one of his own: "Trevor, is your God gloomy?"

His gentle question scorched its way into the depths of my mind and heart. Looking back now, I can see that it opened up significant new directions in my own thinking and living. However, before exploring this more fully, let me share my memories of my first meeting with Dallas. It was because of what he taught me through his own joyfulness that I was willing to take seriously what he taught about the joyous God.

OUR FIRST MEETING

In 1985, I got sick with mumps. While recuperating in bed I came across an audiotape series of talks that Dallas had given the year before at an Africa Enterprise conference in the South African city of Pietermaritzburg. I had not heard of Dallas before. But something in those teachings struck a deep responsive chord in me. As I listened to him explore the themes of the accessibility of the kingdom of God, the substantiality of the spiritual, and the connections between discipleship, daily life and mission, my longing to know, love and follow Jesus burst into stronger flame.

I also knew that I wanted to spend time with this man. So I posted a handwritten letter, introducing myself and inviting him to come again to South Africa to share life with us and to teach in a number of different settings. I said that I could raise his airfare, but could not offer hotel accommodation or promise any substantial honorarium. It was certainly not an attractive offer. To my surprise and delight, Dallas responded positively to this request from a complete stranger. Nor did we, he said, have to worry about any payment.

In August 1987, Dallas endured the twenty-five hour air trip from Los Angeles and landed at the Johannesburg airport. His three weeks were spent ministering in Cape Town, Kempton Park and Johannesburg. But what struck me most during this time were not his words. It was his life in our midst. Dallas lived in the house of his own teaching. He was attentive to whoever was speaking with him. He listened carefully to our concerns in South Africa. He prayed for individuals between his teaching sessions. After we gave him an honorarium at the conference, I learned from a colleague working in an impoverished area that Dallas had given him the money!

And then there was his joyfulness. Whether it was listening to him singing on his own a favorite hymn, or catching him in his room delighting in photographs of Jane, Becky and John, or overhearing him talking with the Lord in our lounge at midnight, or standing quietly with him as the sun set over the lake, or watching him play with our young children or enjoying a beer and spicy grilled chicken after a long day of ministry, I noticed a contagious joy about his presence. Thinking about this now, I realize that it was because of Dallas's embodied sense of overall well-being that his question carried such weight and authority, demanding from me serious thought, study and reflection. Engaging it led me to rethink my picture of God and to reshape my way of life. Both of these changes became part of my journey into joy.

RETHINKING MY PICTURE OF GOD

Our picture of God is critical in a number of respects. First of all, it profoundly affects the way we relate to God. If we have a vague, fuzzy and impersonal picture of God, then our relationship with God usually turns out to be vague, fuzzy and impersonal. Or if we picture God to be against us or always out to get us, it will be highly unlikely that we will want to get too intimate with God. Or if we feel that we have to earn God's love, then we will spend our lives huffing and puffing trying to put ourselves into God's good books. How we understand God influences powerfully the nature of our relationship with God.

But there is another reason why our picture of God is so important. Our picture of God rubs off on us. We become like the God we worship. If we believe that God is violent, we will tend toward aggression. If we understand God to be against certain people, we will be opposed to them as well. If we see God as overly serious, we will most probably come across as heavy ourselves. It would seem that we shape our picture of God and then that picture of God shapes us.

For many years prior to the moment when Dallas asked me that question, I had been thinking through my picture of God. From painful, personal experience, I knew that much of our pain in life comes from our failure to think rightly about God. Thanks to the companionship of a wonderful psychiatrist, I had already been on a gradual journey from understanding God as someone whose love had to be earned to understanding God as someone who loved me unconditionally. Now Dallas's question was causing another significant shift in my understanding of God to take place within me.

I started by going back to the gospel life of Jesus. The bottom line of the Christian faith is the amazing claim that God has stepped into human history in the person of Jesus. If we want to get our picture of God clearer we need to continually look in the direction of Jesus. Through word and deed, dying and rising, Jesus introduces us to what God really is. With Dallas's question echoing in my memory, I began to follow Jesus again through the Gospels, seeking this time to notice what I had missed before.

I already knew that according to Isaiah 53:3, Jesus was "a man of sorrows, and acquainted with grief" (ESV)—the compassionate friend who wept at Lazarus's tomb, the vulnerable Savior who grieved over Jerusalem when entering the city riding on a donkey, the crucified one who experienced the darkness of God-forsakenness. These images dominated my theology. Around them I developed my understanding of the God who always suffers with us in our suffering, weeps with us in our tears and grieves with us in our grief. But now I knew that I needed to allow other images of Jesus to take their rightful place in my picture of God.

During my rereading of the Gospels, I was struck by how happy Jesus was. He lived with a strong, vibrant sense of the goodness of his Father, the Creator of the world. He seemed to have had the capacity of living fully in the present, giving his attention to the task in front of him, celebrating the presence of God here and now. He enjoyed parties, sharing meals, hugging children. He loved those around him fiercely and passionately. To cap it off, after explaining to his disciples how he would be the vine and they the branches, constantly drawing life from him, he said, "These things I have

spoken to you, that my joy may in you, and that your joy may be full"
(Jn 15:11 ESV).

Gradually, through this fresh seeing of the Gospels' portrait of
Jesus, I found myself becoming receptive to the idea of the joyous
God. I began to imagine for the first time the joy that God must
constantly experience—the joy in creating this expanding universe,
the joy in continuously experiencing everything that is good and
beautiful, the joy in loving you and me each moment of our lives. I
also came to see that affirming the joy in God did not have to mean
denying God's presence in our suffering. I was beginning to understand that God is both the God of the crucified Jesus *and* the God
of the risen Jesus.

This re-visioning of God initiated significant changes for me. I
started regularly to ask God to fill my life with the joy of Jesus. Inwardly, I gave myself permission to be happy even in the midst of
painful circumstances. I began to see more clearly that if I was going
to weep with those who weep and rejoice with those who rejoice, I
needed to be able to hold both these things together in myself. I even
allowed myself the delightful thought that I brought joy to God.

RESHAPING MY DAILY LIFE

Even after my ideas about a gloomy God started to change, there
were still times when I would get very down. I knew enough about
genuine character formation to realize that I could not sit back and
expect God to fill my life with joy while I did nothing. Some careful
thought would need to be given to how I could reshape my daily life
in order to open my life to the joy of God.

Again Dallas was very helpful. On one occasion, after I had
written to him describing my deeply ingrained struggle to embrace
joy more fully, I received back a letter with wise and practical direction. Not only did his words communicate a kind acceptance of
who I was, they also offered me some clues regarding what I could
do to receive more fully the joy of Jesus. Here is one paragraph from

that letter.

> Being discontent and always halfway disappointed is a part of
> what you are as a pilgrim on the earth. You are always going to
> feel like "arrangements," whether family, church or state, even
> children, are sawdust and not bread. Very likely it derives from
> something—not "bad"—in your early experiences that formed
> your feelings and sentiment and left a gap in your sensitivities.
> Something it would take a revelation from God to make you
> know, and which you could do nothing about if you did know.
> Introspectiveness is part of your nature. It is not bad. Don't
> fight it. Find sources of joy and cultivate them. Invest in them:
> time and money. . . . What things do you really enjoy? Things
> that have nothing to do with family, work or religion.[2]

I frequently return to these words. They have helped me to see
how I can think and live in a way more conducive to experiencing
God's joy. Let me explore three shifts in my thinking and living that
continue to this day.

Celebrating more joyfully my own existence. Dallas's spiritual
direction got me thinking in a different way about my own life.
Somehow, his words encouraged me to celebrate my existence in
this universe more joyfully. I didn't need to fight the person I was.
Being discontent and always halfway disappointed was part of who
I was as a pilgrim on the earth. It did not mean that God had done
badly with me or that there was something wrong with me or that
I was inferior to any other person. God genuinely delighted in me!
I could accept myself as I was.

Thinking about my life in this way has required much grace. We
live in a world intent on getting us to be constantly dissatisfied with
our lives. After all, how else would they sell us all that stuff! Often
the voices around us telling us that we are not acceptable are very
loud. Almost daily, we need the Holy Spirit to assure us in our
hearts that we have been loved by God into existence. I have been

learning to ask each time I pray for the grace to know more deeply that when God looks at me, God says, "I did well in giving you life. I did not make a mistake. You bring a smile to my face."

Developing a celebrative lifestyle. By inviting me to invest time and money in sources of joy, I believe that Dallas was encouraging me to explore the neglected spiritual discipline of celebration. In one place, he describes spiritual celebration in this way: "We engage in celebration when we enjoy ourselves, our life, our world, *in conjunction with* our faith and confidence in God's greatness, beauty, and goodness."[3] Biblically grounded in the book of Leviticus, where the people of God are instructed to set apart a tithe of their yearly produce, transport it to Jerusalem and enjoy a feast in the Lord's presence, celebration was a practice of which I had little firsthand experience.

But I began to learn to reshape my life here as well. Mealtimes became important daily celebrations where family and friends could share in conversation and laugh together; family birthdays and anniversaries were turned into occasions for fun and thanksgiving; weekends away with Debbie at special places refreshed us in our love for each other. As I did these things, I consciously sought to enter into the joy of God who I now knew was also enjoying these moments with me. Not surprisingly, after times like these I would often feel nourished in my faith and strengthened to take up the responsibilities of my daily life with greater love and joy.

Finding God in all things. Then, Dallas's counsel was intriguingly non-spiritual. There was no word to me about praying more, studying the Bible more, praising God more. While I knew that these activities were critically important for him, his approach to my predicament was much more indirect. I believe it also expressed his deep conviction that he once shared with me at another time: "Religion must never become your life. Your life needs to become your religion." In the words of St. Ignatius, Dallas wanted me to learn how to experience God in all things, especially those things I enjoyed.

Overcoming this split between sacred and secular has perhaps turned out to be my deepest avenue of joy. I do not have to pepper my conversation all day long with religious expressions of praise and thanksgiving. What I can do is enter the present moment fully, live it as deeply as I can and know God's presence in it. After all, when I invite people over to a meal that I have prepared, what brings me most joy is not when my guests praise me for what I have cooked yet only nibble at it, but when they enjoy the meal and ask for more! Surely the same is true with God and God's precious gift of life to each of us.

Because of the journey Dallas's question initiated for me, I now regard joy as a primary foundation of life in the kingdom of God. This joy flows from the vision of God as the most joyous being in the universe. Not only does God want to give us this joy; we need to constantly seek it as well. Joy does not automatically happen to us. But knowing that the risen Christ has decisively overcome the powers of darkness and death, and that nothing can ultimately separate us from the reality of God's loving presence, we can learn how to choose joy and so become one of those joyous Christ followers who heal, transform and bless our suffering world.

Trevor Hudson is a minister in the Methodist Church of Southern Africa, presently serving in the Northfield Methodist Church, Benoni, South Africa. His two most recent books are *Discovering Our Spiritual Identity* (InterVarsity Press) and *Holy Spirit Here and Now* (Upper Room).

DALLAS WILLARD, EVANGELIST

Todd Hunter

I have had a lifelong interest in, and frustration with, evangelism. As a teenage convert I thought it would be ultra cool to be the next Billy Graham. I would have settled for being the next Greg Laurie—the popular and effective evangelist of Harvest Crusade fame in Southern California, through whose ministry I came to faith. In particularly discouraging moments, I've thought, *Of all the people in the world who most love evangelism, I may be the least good at it!*

Thus you'll understand my accompanying thirst to learn all I could about the gospel and how to effectively proclaim it so that my hearers would come to faith. Dallas's book *The Divine Conspiracy* was the major impetus for my doctor of ministry dissertation. Its title was "Rehearing the Gospel Towards Improved Practices in Evangelism and Discipleship."

Along this hungry path of learning and growth, from a naive but enthusiastic teenager to a professor of evangelism and contemporary culture, I have studied the major evangelists and their presentations. I once owned and read most of Graham's sermons. I sought to train myself in all things gospel related so that I could contextualize and articulate the best interpretation of the gospel I possibly could in American culture.

Along the way I discovered a lot of evangelists who tried to scare people away from their sins and hell while offering forgiveness and heaven in exchange for saying a prayer. No knock on them. Hell, whatever exactly it is, will be brutal and should be avoided at all costs. And heaven, whatever amazing reality it turns out to be, will be indescribably great and should be sought at all costs. So far so good.

But in my view something went really wrong when a reductionist version of that gospel got married to the American marketing machine. My point is not that marketing is inherently evil or that it must never be used in gospel enterprises. Rather, I believe that what the last few decades of evangelistic ministry teach us about the marriage of gospel and marketing is rooted in the law of unintended consequences.

Marketing by its very definition requires sound bites suitable to the pace of talk shows, taglines that fit on billboards and sayings that can be displayed on bumper stickers. This squishing of the gospel for marketing reasons is what gave us the memorable 1970s bumper sticker, "Christians aren't perfect, just forgiven." Really? *Just* forgiven? That's all there is to the big story of God? A more current sticker that I believe is misleading is "Not of this world!" I know what the text says: Jesus' kingdom is not of this world (Jn 18:36). I think I know what it means: Jesus' kingdom derives from his Father and is owned and operated for his Father's divine purposes, not the political, economic or ethnic factions that consistently fought Jesus during his ministry. But it does *not* mean what the backs of cars seem to imply: *I* am not of this world—as if I should have nothing to do with this sinful world.

This cannot be the case because just a few pages later in John's Gospel, Jesus is quoted saying, "As the Father has sent me [into the world], I am sending you" (Jn 20:21 NIV). On and on, from "the Fish

Wars" (images of the Christian fish eating the Darwin fish), to present-day tweets, Snapchats and Instagram photos and beyond, these reductionisms have flourished and misshaped the minds and hearts of millions of Americans who think they have heard the gospel according to Jesus, but in fact have not.

A Fresh Hearing for Jesus

Into this reductionist scene came Dallas Willard, who began the introduction to his award-winning book *The Divine Conspiracy* with these words: *"My hope is to gain a fresh hearing for Jesus."*[1] That is the heart of an evangelist. I realize most people think of Dallas as an esteemed philosopher. I do too. He introduced me to the literature of epistemology so I could learn to contend for the gospel in the midst of postmodern angst regarding truth. I know his students loved him as a teacher. As an informal student, I did too. But look at those italicized words again: they focus and leverage the philosopher and teacher traits of Dallas into the passion of a true evangelist.

On more than one occasion I heard Dallas refer to himself as "essentially a Southern Baptist evangelist." Or he'd say, "I've always just thought of myself as what I was when I was a young Southern Baptist—an evangelist." Hearing this always made me tilt my head a bit because I knew that Dallas and his wife, Jane, had for many years been meaningfully involved in the Valley Vineyard church in Reseda, California, led by my longtime friend Bill Dwyer. Furthermore, Dallas never spoke or acted like many Southern Baptists I have known over my decades in ministry.

Recalling those moments as I write this, I don't think Dallas meant for the accent to be on the *Baptist* part. He certainly was never critical of his Baptist upbringing, and I'm not implying any criticism of Baptists here. But Dallas's accent was on the *evangelist* part. It seemed Dallas was trying to say something like, "When I was a young man I loved getting a hearing for Jesus. I still do."

In my considered view, Dallas proclaimed the gospel according to Jesus better than any evangelist of the twentieth and early twenty-first centuries. I may be wrong, and I'd be happy to be otherwise enlightened, but I mean it. I am not just saying this to honor Dallas's memory in a book devoted to him. I sincerely think I am right. Dallas Willard, in contrast to the reductionist gospels so often heard today, preached a gospel of life in the kingdom now, "a life that has the quality of eternity,"[2] a life that never ends and that deals with our sins, too.

The first few chapters of *The Divine Conspiracy* contain a withering critique of the most popular "gospels" of Dallas's lifetime. First, Dallas demonstrates how the gospel on the left, the call to eliminate social injustice as defined in any given point in human history, is included in but does not reach the fullness of the gospel of Jesus. Nor has it proven to make disciples of Jesus.

The gospel on the right does not do much better. *Say this prayer so that when you die you can go to heaven* does not match the gospel of Jesus or routinely succeed at making disciples either. It has generated endless debates about atonement theory, definitions of justification and so on. But the reductionist gospel says little to nothing about ecclesiology (What does it mean to be the people of God?), missiology (What is the mission of God and how does it relate to the church?) or pneumatology (Who is the Holy Spirit? And what place does the Spirit have in a reductionist story about the Son placating an angry Father?). Radically abridged accounts of the gospel combined with the rationalistic, scientific, empirical Western worldview all but relegated the person and work of the Spirit to the mustiest dustbin of human history: crazy superstition.

But let's reverse all that through a gospel story derived from the words of Jesus in Mark 1:15. The gospel according to Jesus sets us on a completely different trajectory: "Review your plans for living [repent] and base your life on this remarkable new opportunity [believe]"[3] to live "an eternal kind of life now."[4] That message of Jesus alerts us to a different kind of life in the new, reconstituted people of God (ecclesiology); to being the cooperative friends of Jesus, living lives of constant creative goodness for the sake of others (missiology); through the authority, power, gifts and character transformation of the Holy Spirit (pneumatology).

Dallas definitely won a new hearing for Jesus in me. *The Divine Conspiracy* fell to my lap with a thud when I, the one compelled by my lifelong evangelistic frustration, finished reading this concise, powerfully persuasive sentence: "What message would we preach that would naturally lead to a decision to become an apprentice of Jesus in The Kingdom Among Us?"[5]

I read that powerful sentence as a question directed to me (and later heard Dallas say it to groups of ministers this way): *Does the gospel I teach and preach routinely lead my hearers to become followers of Jesus?*

It was a long time before I lifted the book up from my lap. And that sentence, well marked and starred, arrests my attention every time I see it. I linger over it in prayer asking God to give me the ability to do just that: preach and teach the gospel of Jesus such that people see its beauty, power and goodness and then give themselves to Jesus as his apprentice.

A new hearing for Jesus was leading me to a new view of the person of Jesus as well. I was coming to see Jesus as something more than the source of blood to cover my sins (though his blood does do that). Becoming increasingly clear to me was a view of Jesus as a person worthy of our deepest love, admiration and respect. The next step for me was to connect this *new* Jesus to the work of evangelism.

A NEW VIEW OF JESUS

"Our usual 'gospels' are, in their effects—dare we say it—nothing less than a standing invitation to *omit* God from the course of our daily existence."[6] There goes the book again—down on my lap. It was as if I needed to focus all my bodily strength on thinking, so

much so that I couldn't even hold a book! A thought like that
changes everything in the heart and mind of a frustrated evangelist
like me looking for the right ways to do things. Not willing to abide
the reality of an *omitted* Christ, Dallas Willard consistently argued
in his speaking, teaching and writing for the brilliance of Jesus
against the "misunderstanding of Jesus that treats him as nice but
not very intelligent." Dallas knew this misunderstanding to be the
"death knell of discipleship."[7]

Thus Dallas constantly set Jesus before us as a person of abundant
ability, "the unrivaled master of human life,"[8] and thus worthy of
our esteem, of placing our confidence in him and following him,
"surrendering the inmost reality of [ourselves] to God as expressed
in Jesus and his kingdom."[9] Through Dallas's ministry, scores of my
colleagues, hundreds of my friends and countless thousands of
others did indeed receive a new picture of Jesus and were *re-converted*, so to speak, to Jesus and his kingdom message.

Who Is Your Teacher?

For Dallas, no evangelistic question in all of life was more transformative, more direction setting than, "Who teaches you? Whose
disciple are you? Honestly." For "one thing is sure," Dallas wrote,
"you are somebody's disciple. You [are learning] how to live from
somebody else. There are no exceptions to this rule."[10] Dallas insisted that authentic faith in Jesus includes at its core the gospel
about Jesus—his death and resurrection for us and for our sins—
but that it cannot be reduced to this. We also need to hear, take
seriously and place our confidence in the gospel *of* Jesus, seen in
passages such as Matthew 4:17 and Mark 1:14-15.

Our faith in Jesus has to include being his students or apprentices: we "learn from Jesus how to live our life as he would live it if
he were we."[11] For Dallas, such *followership of Jesus* into living in
the kingdom is the good life, life as God intended for human
beings. Putting it quite straightforward in *The Divine Conspiracy,*

Willard wrote: "It is a main purpose of this book on Jesus and his kingdom to help us face this fact of the absence of Jesus as teacher and to change it."[12] Dallas wanted us to deeply appreciate and value, in more than a notional way, Jesus' teachings and Jesus' way of being in the world. He wanted to enlarge our view of Jesus beyond merely a source of blood in the context of an arrangement to have our sins forgiven by an angry God. Dallas wanted his hearers to come to know in a self-authenticating way—in the manner in which the Gospel of John sets forth the whole breadth of Jesus' reality in our lives—how who Jesus is matches the greatest needs of humanity: the Bread of Life—my real sustenance; the Light of the world—lighting my path; the Gate—opening God's kingdom to me; the Good Shepherd—allowing me to live free of the clutches of wanting; and the Way, the Truth and the Life—the one in whom I can place so much confidence that I would give myself to doing as he says is best.

This kind of experiential, self-authenticating knowledge was crucial to Dallas. He never meant to say that doctrinal or systematic ways of knowing are somehow bad—they're just incomplete in a big way. Dallas knew that humanity in general and even many Christians were, without conscious awareness of it, "flying upside down."[13] He believed that a sole focus on the afterlife was causing people to ignore God's provision for this life. Thus he evangelized everyone he could not just into a secure death, as important as that is, but also into *a new way of life* grounded in following Teacher Jesus.

"I make bold to say," Dallas wrote, "[that] the gospel of the entire New Testament is that you can have new life now in the Kingdom of God if you will trust Jesus Christ."[14] He wanted his readers and hearers to do the words of Jesus, to be "'like those intelligent people who build their houses upon rock,' standing firm against every pressure of life (Matt. 7:24-25)."[15] Dallas wanted us, after making Jesus our Master Teacher and carefully attending to his words, to reply: "I will do them! I will find out how. I will devote my life to it! This is the best life strategy I have ever heard of!"[16]

As Dallas taught, this call to a new life should be the core of evangelism:

> Spiritual transformation into Christ-likeness requires a conscious, clearheaded and public commitment to living as a disciple of Jesus Christ; that is, to a decision to give our lives to him as his constant students, learning from him how to live all aspects of our lives as he would live them. *Evangelism should be understood as a call to receive the gift of such a life.*[17]

NOT JUST BELIEF, COMMITMENT OR PROFESSION, BUT KNOWLEDGE

For Dallas, at the core of gaining a new hearing for Jesus and making him our Teacher is moving past mere religious *belief* rooted in surface *commitment* or, even worse, unbelieving *profession*. Dallas preached and taught to help his hearers acquire *knowledge* of Jesus. In his understanding, we truly have knowledge of Jesus "when we are representing [him] (thinking about [him], speaking of [him], treating [him]) as [he] actually is, on an appropriate basis of thought and experience."[18]

Many people in my boomer generation and the generation just after us particularly resonated with Dallas's claim that "an act of faith in the biblical tradition [such as deciding to follow Jesus] is always undertaken in an environment of knowledge and is inseparable from it."[19] For instance, while it is true that Abraham left Ur not knowing where he was going, he did so based on rich interactive knowledge of God and God's care for him. Abraham's ability to move into the unknown was deeply rooted in what was experientially known to him of God.

For Dallas this wasn't an argument for the all-sufficiency of knowledge. He knew, as the apostle Paul did, that knowledge could "puff up" (1 Cor 8:1) and that in this life we only "know in part" (1 Cor 13:8-12). But crucial to Dallas for achieving a new hearing for Jesus was helping people gain confidence in Jesus, and this of course requires sufficient knowledge of him. Far from wanting Christians to have knowledge for arrogant reasons or to dominate others, Dallas wanted humans to have knowledge because "knowledge gives us access to reality."[20]

This was core to Dallas's sense of his work because for him reality was composed of a Triune Being of completely competent love. It is this Triune Being that Willard the evangelist struggled to make plain. For him this was not merely philosophy-speak. It was dead core to what it meant to gain a new hearing for Jesus such that people would actually follow him. For "knowledge of reality tends toward successful and confident interactions with reality."[21] I paraphrase Dallas this way: Knowledge of Jesus tends toward successful and confident interactions with him, toward following him. This is the plain and direct connection between knowledge and evangelism.

Maybe I can help you see the beauty and power of these ideas in a further "Hunter on Willard" way? I have carried his ideas around in my heart and mind for a long time now and have come to think about it like this: Knowledge of the Triune God—a community of Persons who are in their very essence totally competent love—tends toward placing one's confidence in God such that one would choose to and actually follow the final and best earthly expression of God—Jesus the Messiah—and that this positive interaction with God would bear fruit in willing the good of one's neighbor in manifold actions of love, for "love wills the good of what is loved."[22]

That kind of spiritual knowledge and experience is priceless. But I am often asked something like this: "Todd, I know how to preach the simple gospel of the forgiveness of sins, but how do you preach Jesus' more multifaceted gospel of the kingdom?" Let's see if Dallas can help us to do so.

Reclaiming the Word *Discipleship*

Bill Hull

I knew Dallas Willard before I met him. I had read his books and he was my partner in discipleship. I wondered what kind of man he might be.

In 2001 he and I were among a group that had been asked to write papers and discuss the problems that were plaguing the American church. During the first session Dallas made a statement that proved to me he was detached from reality. It was something like, "I am committed to try and not make anything happen."

That evening I slipped into the empty chair next to his and began to ask him about his statement. Since he was a philosopher, I thought I would give him a break and not burst his academic bubble. I started with an easy question: "You make things happen when you write a lecture, when you produce a book, a talk, even when you write an exam. So what do you mean, you don't make anything happen?"

Being a good philosopher, he didn't answer my question directly. He told me that he had abandoned all attempts to get a certain response or create a certain effect when he ministered to others. This came to him, he said, one night while sitting on a platform where he was waiting to speak. He realized that he had no chance to impress or affect the crowd through his talent or skill. He went on to explain to me that doing ministry is like bowling, possibly without the ugly shirt. You do the best you can to roll the ball in the right place, but once you let go there is nothing left to do. No one chases the bowling ball down the alley once the ball is released; all you can do is stand in place and hope it hits something. For Dallas, all the work was in the preparation. "Do good work," he would say, "and the rest is up to God."

The next eleven years were very rich indeed as Dallas and I became friends. Like so many, I felt I was close to him. That was a gift of his—he made all those he spent time with sense he liked them and that he enjoyed their company. I recall one day when he greeted me with, "Bill, I just love thinking about you." As you can tell, I haven't forgotten it.

Another way he affected my ministry is that he slowed me down. I became calmer, more contented and much deeper in both mind and soul.

While I know it would embarrass him, I often think of Dallas as "C. S. Luther," a cross between C. S. Lewis and Martin Luther. Dallas Willard was a bit of both of these men. Like Lewis, he wrote perched in the academy, and this gave his words an eloquence and style that set them apart from the normal language used by Christian writers. His word choices and syntax, with the complete sentences that finished points sharply, were attractive to the educated classes. He believed that if he wrote from the university that the church would remain open to him, and he was right. His thoughts were fresh and carried a certain weight; they had to be taken seriously by the serious.

But perhaps more important, he became like Martin Luther to his generation. While there was no "Here I stand, I can do no other" kind of moment, what he did do was drive a stake into the ground and say, "This is the gospel." And this gospel of the kingdom is not what we have been preaching for the last one hundred years.

Dallas taught that Christ's commission to make disciples is all we have been authorized to do; everything else is a sideshow. As I write, for the first time in my lifetime of ministry we are seeing the importance of discipleship to the church's work. There is a consensus church wide that we must attend to the business of making disciples as the first priority. I attribute this sea change as much to Dallas Willard as to any other person.

Bill Hull is the author of The Disciple Making Pastor, The Complete Book of Discipleship, Christlike, Choose the Life *and many other books on discipleship and the Christian experience.*

DALLAS WILLARD GIVES AN ALTAR CALL

Most altar calls come to an intense and dramatic culmination with these words: If you died tonight, do you know for sure you would go to heaven? As I've already said, life-after-death issues are important. I have no argument with that. But that dramatic question alone has now proven, over long use, to not routinely make disciples of Jesus. Placing all the emphasis on what happens when we die inadvertently presents a standing invitation to *omit* Christ from the course of our daily existence.

We need some better evangelistic questions. Maybe these work better: What if you knew you were going to live tomorrow? What would you do? What story would be the chief orienting force in your life? Who would you follow? Who would be your teacher? Would you like your life to be marked by a richly interactive personal relationship that is the basis of and constitutes a new kind of life—"life from above"?[23] (see Jn 17:3).

Dallas never stood and preached on stages erected in the great stadiums of the modern world—as wonderful as such events can be. Dallas, by divine design, carried out his non-writing work, with the notable exceptions of some large conferences, in the relative quiet of the classroom and the Sunday school room. But had he been in that kind of spotlight, the major news networks of the world picking up and broadcasting his preaching, something like this is undoubtedly the core message that he would have proclaimed:

"In the Gospels . . . 'the gospel' is the good news of the presence and availability of life in the kingdom, now and forever, through reliance on Jesus the Anointed."[24]

Perhaps tonight, having considered the claims of Jesus and the story about Jesus, you are ready to make a choice for him and are wondering what such a decision might mean.

Well, "to know Christ in the modern world is to know him in your world now. To know him in your world now is to live interactively with him right where you are *in your daily activities. This is the* spiritual life *in Christ. He is, in fact, your contemporary, and he is now about* his *business of moving humanity along toward its destiny in this amazing universe. You don't want to miss out on being a part—*your *part—of that great project. You want to be sure to take your life into his life, and in that way to find your life to be 'eternal,' as God intended it."²⁵*

So tonight I am going to ask you, each one of you, all over this great stadium, not to merely recite a prayer outlining one metaphor of the atonement, but rather I'm going to ask you to commit, via the saving power of Christ's cross and the regenerating power of the Holy Spirit, to beginning a new life of "firsthand interaction—*knowing by acquaintance—direct awareness of [Jesus] and his kingdom."²⁶ I am asking you to take up the amazing opportunity to strive first for the kingdom of God and to learn from Jesus that everything else in life will be taken care of.*

Tonight I am asking you to pay attention to Jesus, for he "transcends all social visions and all entanglements with religion."²⁷ *He is present right now in your world, living the most glorious life possible. Tonight I encourage you to* "venture on the kingdom of God and its King," *for* "everyone who calls on the name of Lord shall be saved" *(Acts 2:21).²⁸*

Tonight I am asking you to take Jesus' life into yours, by the grace of God to crucify your present inferior life and pick up Jesus' life instead—and to thereby "steadily grow in graceful interactions with Father, Son, and Holy Spirit. They [will] gradually take up all of [your] life into their trinitarian life (John 17:21-24)."²⁹ *In so doing you will become humanity as God intended, with a never-ceasing future as God's cooperative friends in the new heaven and new earth.*

I can hear some of you saying in your hearts, But Dallas, I've tried religion, attended church and dabbled in the Bible—it didn't work for me! *I know and I empathize with you. But there is a simple explanation for your frustration: When the walk with Christ does not work, it is "because* we do not give ourselves to it in a way that allows our lives to be taken over by it."[30]

So rather than religion or church, as good as they may be, tonight I am asking you to do something markedly different. I am asking you to make the decision to trust and follow Jesus. I am asking you to "enroll as his disciple."[31]

In a moment I'm going to ask you to make this decision. If you do, your sins will be forgiven through Jesus' atoning death on the cross and you will be converted—that is, you will have taken the first step of being ushered by God's grace and power into a completely new life, realizing God's purpose for which he created you: that you would be a "never-ceasing spiritual being with a unique eternal calling to count for good in God's great universe."[32]

Will you do it? Will you enroll as Jesus' apprentice? Will you trust and follow Jesus?

Bishop Todd D. Hunter leads Churches for the Sake of Others, a church-planting initiative of the Anglican Church in North America. He is the author of a number of books, including *Christianity Beyond Belief.*

14

DEVELOPING PASTORS AND CHURCHES OF THE KINGDOM

Alan Fadling

Fifteen years ago, Dallas Willard was the speaker for two days with a community of about seventy-five pastors who were alumni of the first four cohorts of The Leadership Institute's Journey program.[1] *The Divine Conspiracy* had just been released, and many of us were devouring it. Dallas spoke on expected themes like abiding in Christ and the value of spiritual disciplines. He also addressed "Developing a Theology and Models of the Church" and "Hope for Living Godly in a Postmodern Age," which especially targeted our focus on inspiring generations of leaders who listen to God, follow Jesus' rhythms of life and extend his kingdom out of the overflow of their intimacy with God.

I often heard (or overheard) Dallas express concern about anything that would function as a tribute to him or, worse, result in the emergence of some sort of Willardite movement. My hope is that we see Dallas's life and writings as signposts pointing the way to Christ and his kingdom. While in this book many have expressed appreciation for what they learned about spiritual formation or philosophy from Dallas, I would like to share here what I learned from him about godly, spiritual leadership, especially during those two days so many years ago.

I was always impressed by Dallas's lack of self-referencing or self-promotion. It stood out in a church world where it always seemed leaders were looking for recognition. Dallas had a deep security in Jesus that I have found myself also seeking.

Dallas invited us, as pastors, to imagine living among and leading a redeemed people who were as astonished to see someone do wrong as we are currently astonished to see someone do right. It was spending time with Dallas that often made me feel that following Jesus was the most natural thing a pastor might choose to do (as odd as that may sound to some). He turned a way of life that too often felt like an unreachable ideal into a way I could actually come to live.

In my own life as a pastor, and in my work training other pastors, I resonated with Dallas's statement that many of us hold back our twisted impulses for the sake of ministry success (whatever that means), but that such success does not prevent the inevitable breakdowns or sinkholes resulting from poorly tended inner lives. Listening to Dallas built in me the conviction that there may be no greater leadership task than tending one's own growing life of communion with Jesus.

It is this idea of intentional communion with Jesus at the heart of my ministry work that Dallas sharpened for me. Leadership is too often an effort to pump something up rather than letting something flow from within us. What if leadership were one of those things that flowed like rivers of living water through the opening of our simple trust in Jesus (Jn 7:38)?

I came to see that so much of the spiritual influence I hoped to have in God's kingdom was an indirect fruit rather than a direct pursuit. This was where Dallas's focus on classic spiritual disciplines continued to help me. I learned the importance of accepting ambiguity when my leadership instincts usually aim to eliminate the slightest whiff of it—because that instinct can make the church more machine than living organism. People are ambiguous. Communities are unpredictable. I cannot manage the mystery of the spiritual life or the church into a one-size-fits-all, seven-step system. Christian leadership must not be about defining a system that we run at the unintended expense of crushing the life out of people who try to survive in that system.

I also began to experience disciplines such as solitude and silence—which can be so counterintuitive to a busy pastor—as spaces where I learn that my sense of value, influence and importance are not established in all that I do, but rather, all that I do is an expression of who I truly and deeply am in communion with Jesus.

As a pastor, I came to realize how often I was seeking the attention of God's people rather than learning to point them to Jesus. I realized that my great opportunity was to help others learn that they could come to Jesus not only in the relatively few minutes we gathered week to week, but in the hundreds of minutes we were scattered back into our homes, neighborhoods and workplaces. I saw how tempted I was to make myself the focus of attention rather than being content, as I often felt Dallas was, to simply be a pointer toward the way to the King.

I suppose the greatest leadership insight Dallas gave me was that pastors and Christian leaders have two main means of causality (which I read as influence): direct and prayerful. I put so much weight on what I do directly when I'm speaking, counseling, planning or implementing. But God is the only one who can deal directly with the inner lives of people. I don't have that kind of direct access. So prayer became for me a critical opportunity for spiritual influence. Along these lines, I began to see how many of Paul the apostle's prayers are much more about soul issues than situation issues.

As an illustration, Dallas asked us why we thought Jesus prayed for Peter rather than just fixing him. He said that Jesus knew such fixing was a job that needed to be left up to his Father. There are certainly things we have direct power to affect, but the changing of people's inner lives is something in which we would do better to cooperate with the Father through our prayerful care for others.

The way Dallas affirmed the power of a changing life was to remind us that what God treasures in someone's life is the person they become more than the work that they do. Dallas reminded us that the deepest ministry we have with others is who we are more than what we say or do.[2]

It is the continuing simplicity of living our lives in communion with Jesus by following the way of Jesus that I hope we all will take from our encounters with Dallas, whether in person or in his writings. This is, as Thomas Kelly called it, the simplicity of the trusting child—the simplicity that lies beyond complexity. It is a simplicity that is the beginning of spiritual maturity.[3]

My hope is that we can continue to allow the beauty and simplicity of Jesus among us to draw us into places of deeper rootedness in him, and to engage the simple spiritual disciplines Dallas recommended rather than merely reading another book about them. Perhaps this book will help many to take one little next step, like planting a seed, followed by more small steps, like watering that seed. Over time, perhaps many of us would find ourselves living lives that display the beauty of Jesus in ways similar to those that seem to radiate from the life of Dallas Willard.

Alan Fadling is the executive director of The Leadership Institute (www .spiritualleadership.com), which seeks to inspire generations of leaders who listen to God, follow Jesus' rhythms of life and extend his kingdom out of the overflow of their intimacy with God. Alan is the author of *An Unhurried Life.*

15

GRAY'S ANATOMY AND THE SOUL

Mindy Caliguire

Many years ago, following a traumatic season of "forced rest," I became convinced that I needed to care for my soul. I had no clear sense of what the soul even was, but I knew mine needed help. Though it was "saved," it was certainly *not* well with my soul. My soul had withered from severe neglect as I worked so very hard to help the ministry I served in succeed.

In my exasperation and frustration, I actually had to learn *not* to care about everything happening in ministry around me. If I could simply focus on caring for my soul, I reasoned, God could do through me whatever he wanted.

How did I care for my soul? I prayed in new ways. I found spaces for silence and solitude. I opened up more authentically to those around me. I enjoyed the simple tasks of being a mom, living in the moment, practicing peace.

SOUL WISDOM

More than seven years later, while working on the staff of Willow

Creek in the field of spiritual formation, I was challenged by John Ortberg to read Dallas Willard's newest book, *Renovation of the Heart*. What a gift!

I discovered inside these pages the philosophical, biblical and even theological framework in which I could finally *understand* what I experienced. *This is how a soul is cared for!*

The human soul, designed by God, invisibly drives everything—integrating all dimensions of personhood—and we need to learn to hear its cries; we need to learn how to place it solidly in the care of God. And through the grace we receive in the care of God, we are formed, or re-formed, ever so gradually into the character, or likeness, of Jesus.

I felt I had been given the definitive anatomy book for the soul—a *Gray's Anatomy* for the soul. Here are a few of my favorite quotes about the soul from *Renovation of the Heart*:

> Fundamental aspects of life such as art, sleep, sex, ritual, family ("roots"), parenting, community, health, and meaningful work all are in fact soul functions, and they fail and fall apart to the degree that soul diminishes.[1]

> When we speak of the human soul, then, we are speaking of the *deepest level of life and power* in the human being.[2]

Viscerally, I knew this to be true. But here was *Dallas Willard* affirming that, by God's design, the soul drives everything that matters to us. What we do with this reality is multifaceted. First, of course, it affects my life as an individual. But while I bear that responsibility alone, I do not live alone. I live in the context of others. In fact, an entire dimension of my personhood, Dallas taught, is my social context—the way I relate to others. My soul is not simply a "me and God" thing. It is inherently communal, crafted in the communal image of the trinitarian God.

Beyond my immediate context of relationships, the central

question my friends and I began asking was quite simple: *How could the soul health and transformation available to us become normative in our experience as a church community?* While such experience of soul transformation has certainly been normative in seasons throughout history and even today, it is largely absent, or at least rare and idiosyncratic, in many environments where I have served.

MINISTRY WISDOM

Dallas wrote and taught much on this topic of soul care, both on the possibility for communities to live into this vision and on the tragic consequences of its absence. Personally I became frustrated at times with so much "leadership" focus in the church. Is leadership development really our biggest challenge? Really? How will that improve our ability to help people find the path of life as disciples of Jesus? Is that what we are leading toward?

As I got to know Dallas over the past ten years, I would at times voice my (immature) frustration. Would things in the church around the world ever really change toward a kingdom perspective? Would we really see a shift? What difference could I possibly make?

Dallas challenged me. Gently, of course. But firmly and clearly. He strongly affirmed the vital role church leaders would need to play in facilitating the kind of change desired. He challenged me to hold fast to my idealism for how the church could or should be, and at the same time look straight in the face of the very real obstacles to bringing about that change. Through his teaching and writing and in conversation, I learned how Dallas could articulate both error and opportunity. He could articulate how to not shrink back from what needed to change, nor to ever, ever, *ever* lose hope that God's loving, powerful and grace-filled intentions would prevail. How to provide wisdom for the way forward, not a snarky sideline critique.

He challenged me to love, bless and serve church leaders whenever possible. To stay engaged. Any despair, handwringing, disengagement, judgment, anger or elitism violates, quite strongly, the very changes he espoused. These were not the way of Jesus, nor the way of Dallas.

Ministry Soul

One of Dallas's greatest gifts to me personally was his repeated, if simple, challenge to place *my* confidence in the reality of the kingdom. Duh. With the topics that might make me most anxious on any given day—whether it's the changes I long to see in the complex and overwhelming world around me (there are many), or the changes I long to see in the complex and overwhelming world within me (often way harder)—I can rest in God's care. Shoulders down. My soul is well. He is at work, and all will be well.

Whatever part I have to play in this world, I will do it with all the intensity and passion I have to offer. But not with more than I have to offer. And having made my offering, I can let go of the outcomes. I can rest. I can both care and not care.

I am learning to hold fast both to the reality of the kingdom and the reality of this world into which Jesus has called my name.

And yours. Hold fast.

An Essential Path for Leaders

One of the ideas from *Renovation of the Heart* that most helped me personally and in my work is from a small section in chapter eight, "Transforming the Will." Dallas describes this transformation as a progression that happens to us as we mature (if we mature).

We move, Dallas wrote, from surrender to drama.

In the end, this simple framework has helped me continue to rest my own soul in the care of God as he leads me into different facets of *his* work, not mine.

In *surrender*, we only yield to God's ways after a bit of a fight. We finally cry "uncle" when pinned. But as we begin to trust the inverted logic of the kingdom, we move to a stage marked by *abandonment*, where we sense the difference between God's ways and our ways and more willingly abandon ourselves to God's ways.

In *contentment*, we experience everything in life as happening in the context of a God who is active in this world, who is fundamentally good and who can be trusted. Come what may, we rest content.

But even deeper still, Dallas suggested a stage that ancient writers described as union with God: *participation*. In this stage, disciples of Jesus are most alert and responsive to the movements of God, and most dead to their own agenda and ego. These are the people whose faith moves mountains. Who become agents of grace. Who are truly used by God, but are in no way used up by God.

Unfortunately, we often take new believers with strong leadership potential and thrust them into significant roles without having allowed their inner character to be re-formed by this essential process.

I believe our only hope for leaders to increasingly work in the way of Jesus, for the glory of Jesus, in the power of Jesus and under the direction of Jesus will be as they have passed through stages that help them learn the soul work of surrender, abandonment, contentment and participation. There simply are no shortcuts.

This is what I hope to become—and what I want the body of Christ to be for our world.

Mindy Caliguire is the founder and president of Soul Care, a spiritual formation ministry. She has worked with both churches and organizations such as the Willow Creek Association to encourage leadership and soul development of individuals and congregations. Her writing includes the Soul Care series: *Discovering Soul Care, Spiritual Friendship, Soul Searching* and *Simplicity.*

16

The Kingdom of God
Is Real

Kent Carlson

I remember very vividly my first encounter with the teachings of Dallas Willard. I was reading his book *In Search of Guidance* (now titled *Hearing God*), and at one point I put the book down, stared off into space for a moment and said out loud so I could taste the words, "Oh my goodness! I just met a man who actually believes in God." Now, I know how silly or trivial that statement might seem to the casual reader. But in the most gracious and profound way, Dallas presented an interactive life with God that was so real, so normal, so "everyday-ish" that it made all the religious talk I had been steeped in for so many years seem pale, shadowy and almost pretend.

I have an atheistic background. There was a time in my life when I did not believe in God. I lived in a world where God was ultimately unnecessary. Then I had one of those dramatic conversion experiences that thrust me not only into a life with God, but also into a religious subculture that so often seemed to me small, shallow, dull and strange. I felt trapped. If I was going to be a God-follower, this religious subculture seemed like the only show in town. Yet I felt I could not share with anybody the often oppressive and profound doubts I had about the whole thing. I believed I had, in some way, made contact with God, or he with me, but the current cultural religious expression of my faith fell horribly short of what I believed in my bones a life with God would be like. In secret and unspoken parts of myself I harbored the horrible thought that perhaps everything I believed was a lie. If God were real, certainly a life with him should be experienced as grander, more enthralling and intellectually and spiritually captivating. Yet that was not my experience. Usually I assumed the problem lay with me. At other, darker times I feared the whole thing was a sham.

Then I encountered the teachings of Dallas Willard. Dallas's captivating and enthralling vision of our life with God dismantled and rebuilt my understanding of God and his ways. Dallas taught me how to believe in God again. He spoke about our life with God in a manner that often made me laugh with joy, thinking to myself, "It's all true, isn't it? There really is a God and he is wonderful!" Dallas, some fifteen years after my conversion experience, introduced me to Jesus Christ. I was never the same again.

Dallas had a childlike, playful innocence about his life with God. He saw every person he met as "an unceasing spiritual being with an eternal destiny in God's great universe." He was a rigorous intellectual and academic who never played the game of cynicism. He saw cynicism as intellectual laziness.

He wonderfully embodied Ricoeur's "second naiveté." I was with Dallas once when he prayed for a man's physical ailment. Immediately after the prayer, he held the man by the shoulder and looked at him with hopeful and expectant eyes, and then asked, "Do you feel anything?" I remember being struck by the fact that Dallas fully expected God to do something, and for the briefest moment, when the man said he didn't feel anything, Dallas's face had the expression of a child who finds out he got a shirt for Christmas instead of the fire truck he was hoping for. But then he immediately let it go. He knew there would be more presents.

My encounter with the actual person of Dallas Willard occurred while I was co–senior pastor of a large, attractional, entrepreneurial, seeker church in California. My dear friend and co–senior pastor, Mike Lueken, along with the elders of our church and other leaders, all became infected with this virus of the kingdom of God in our midst. We could not "do church" in the old way. We had to figure out how to reorder our church in such a way that we could give people reliable means by which to learn, in the details of our lives and with the help of the Spirit of God, how to, as Dallas often said, "routinely and easily live as Jesus would if he were us."

This simple, enthralling and radical refocusing of the mission, programming and structure of our church plunged us into a tumultuous decade of change that drastically reduced the size of our church. But a decade later, through the help of God, the DNA of our church has been transformed. We walked away from the trappings of ambition, consumerism and the external models of success and, slowly and laboriously, over a long and difficult decade, came to embrace, as a church family, authentic transformation as a normal and expected focus of church life.

One of the profound privileges of Mike Lueken's and my life is that Dallas Willard was kind and gracious enough to spend many hours during this decade mentoring us and answering the thousands of question we had as to how we could reengineer our church around the reality of the kingdom of God in our midst. I remember one moment while we were driving in a car together and Mike was presenting a rather difficult challenge that he did not feel particularly capable of handling. Dallas looked at Mike, and he literally raised his hand and waved it like a magician in front of his face and said, quite simply, "You can do this, Mike." And in that moment, right there, both Mike and I were convinced that Mike could do it.

A moment later, snapping myself out of this trance Dallas had

Real Change Is Possible

Mike Lueken

Several years ago I was sitting in a restaurant with my good friend Kent Carlson and our friend Dallas Willard. Kent and I were in the midst of a challenging season of leading our congregation through a difficult transition. We wanted to be a church that took seriously Jesus' invitation to experience new life in his kingdom, but the process of becoming that kind of church was harder than we ever imagined.

Dallas graciously agreed to spend some time with us and share his wisdom. Over the years the three of us had several of these conversations, and I look back on them now with gratitude for the opportunity to drink deeply from a man who knew Jesus so well. Dallas's presence, gentleness and teaching routinely forged new ways for me to think about God and envision life with him. The things he said, the way he said them and most especially the way he lived lingered in my heart long after the conversations were finished. They still linger today. When I reread the thick stack of notes from these various discussions, I am still stirred by their depth and hopefulness. On top of all that, Dallas was just really smart, so learning was almost inevitable.

That day in the restaurant, Dallas did what he so frequently did for me and countless others—he reminded me that I could actually be a different person because of Jesus' life and power at work in me. It really could happen. Life really could be different.

put me in, I asked, "What did you do right there? Was that some kind of Jedi mind trick?"

Dallas laughed and said, essentially, "Boys, the kingdom of God is real." That is what I have learned from Dallas. The kingdom of God is real.

In the words of Mark 4:26-28: "This is what the kingdom of God is like. A man scatters seed on the ground. Night and day, whether he sleeps or gets up, the seed sprouts and grows, though he does not know how. All by itself the soil produces grain" (NIV). This, to me, is one of the secrets to the life of Dallas Willard. He continually trusted that the kingdom of God was real, active, operative and advancing all the time. Since this was true, it was not dependent on him or anybody to make it real, active, operative or advancing. Therefore there was no need for worry, anxiety, manipulating, controlling, rushing about or "making it happen." Certainly we are to work, and to work hard. This is neither an invitation to laziness nor to passivity. Rather, it is an invitation to a life lived in actual confidence in God. And this is, indeed, a most excellent life.

Kent Carlson and Mike Lueken are copastors of Oak Hills Church in Folsom, California, and coauthors of *Renovation of the Church.*

17

A Few Dallas-isms That Changed My Life

Keith Meyer

Short, pithy, bite-size chunks of truth so sticky that they get embedded in the mind and heart, and have the effect that when chewed on they just might change your whole life—I call them Dallas-isms. Along with Dallas's books, they have shaped my life, ministry and dreams for impacting lives.

These are some that have stuck with me and produced the most change.

"God will let into his heaven anyone who can stand it"[1]—meaning that if I haven't wanted to live in love here, why would I like it there?

"Grace is opposed to earning, not effort,"[2] challenged my passivity in discipleship and my overblown fear of effort as earning God's love.

"Leave the results to God—don't sweat it,"[3] lifted a terrible burden of trying in the flesh to force results.

"In the end, what God gets out of your ministry . . . is you,"[4] gave me a brand new joy in serving a God who wasn't "using" me but partnering with and transforming me.

Dallas and I share a love for music. One Dallas-ism that he often told me had to do with the shallow and wishful thinking presented in popular rock songs that try to call people to change. I have often heard him lament, "What real hope can we find in the advice for life presented in lyrics like John Lennon's 'Imagine' or 'Peace Train' by James Taylor and the Dixie Chicks?"

I was fascinated by Dallas's command not only of Scripture but also of contemporary culture, and yet I was sure that this time he had it wrong (I grew up in the late 60s and early 70s and think I know rock music). Sheepishly I interjected, "Oh, Dallas, I think 'Peace Train' was by Cat Stevens."

Undeterred, he stated, "Yes, I know that the original was by him but last year a cover was done by Taylor and the Chicks." I checked on it and he was right.

I have learned to trust what Dallas says about almost anything and to put into practice anything and everything he suggests.

SLOWING DOWN, LISTENING TO GOD

Some influential Dallas-isms were visual. I started by imitating his lack of hurry—by going the speed limit in my car! And I didn't use cruise control, wanting to get the slowness into my body and my life. I actually found that I used my time better when not rushing through everything. This was a result of Dallas's admonition, drawn from John Wesley, to "be in haste, but never hurry."[5] I now know I am too hurried when I start to speed.

In response to Dallas's example and teaching of "praying without ceasing," I began to pray over my day's activity in the morning, and then stop before each appointment or task to keep myself ready to hear God and partner with him through the day. I know I am in trouble when I am too busy to start the day with God as my first encounter, to walk alongside him during my whole day and to end the day with him.

SCRIPTURE MEMORY, INTERCEDING FOR OTHERS

After hearing Dallas quote long passages of Scripture from memory and embody their teaching, I started *memorizing* longer passages, such as Colossians 3:1-17; Psalms 103, 130 and 131; and 2 Peter 1:1-10—passages that focus on transformational processes and kingdom outcomes. Then after months of *meditating* on the texts and asking God to make them come true in my life, I try to take the next step of attempting by God's grace to *master* the life change they promise.

This practice so changed the life of one of my seminary students that when he preached from a passage he was memorizing in order to master, his congregation, unaware of his new practice, asked him why his preaching was now so much more powerful and helpful. When I've suggested the practice to churches I have served, small groups started spontaneously forming to simply memorize, meditate on and master Bible passages—without any program hype or organization.

Imitating Dallas and following his soft nudges toward practices that had become evidenced in his life began to make me notice the times in Scripture when Paul invited readers to follow his example and do whatever they saw in his life (1 Cor 11:1; Phil 3:17; 1 Thess 1:6-7).

I also noticed that both Dallas and Paul had a regular practice of interceding for others (see the beginnings and endings of most of Paul's letters), and both unashamedly told others that they were doing so and what they expected God to do in others' lives as a result of their prayers.

I started to prepare sermons, seminary classes and church leadership retreats differently, giving as much time to praying for the results of the Scripture in my life and in my hearers as I did in what normally took all my prep time: exegesis, studying the passage and preparing the message and content itself. The result was a message and ministry that didn't just present truth for more head knowledge and note taking but moved the hearers with conviction and, from their reports, into life change and the habits of discipline required for it.

Embodied Obedience

The great recurring theme that seemed to be Dallas's dream was seeing resurgent spiritual formation efforts result in *embodied obedience* in disciples of Jesus. We often stop short of actual obedience and the training it requires. Because full obedience involves the hard work of rearranging our time and schedules, learning new habits and attitudes, it is easy to think we have grasped Jesus' teaching when its concepts and precepts merely get in our heads. The fact that Jesus really intended obedience to his commands—that he modeled it and trained for it, expecting us to learn to do so as well—was daunting at first and very challenging, but in the end, exhilarating.

Dallas's encouragement that sin could actually become boring and uninteresting, and that obedience was better and easier on us than sin and offered the best possible life, was really good news for those of us who had given up, were faking it or were trying to white knuckle our way to holiness. We can get to the place where it is more unpleasant and harder for us to go into a rage and shake a fist at a driver who cuts us off in traffic than it is to bless them. Embodied obedience isn't easily angered and offended by such behavior but instead is saddened and concerned for the other's good, without having to even struggle with any other reaction—it is just a part of us, second nature.

Dallas believed that discipleship is about being with Jesus and following him into his life, and that life change in groups is more caught than taught. He recognized the power of example to teach in life-on-life interactions. Or as Cardinal John Henry Newman's prayer, prayed each day by Mother Teresa's Sisters of Mercy, says: "Let us preach you, not by words but by our example, *by the catching force*, the sympathetic influence of what we do, the evident fullness of the love our hearts bear to you."[6]

Dallas taught me most powerfully when I observed his gentle answer to a student's or listener's barbed and even rudely worded question—his head bent in deference to those who vehemently disagreed with him, while his arms were held behind his back in vulnerability in spite of the weight of his great intelligence and personality.

Dallas's smile and humor were also catching, and made the shocking but exhilarating vision of life in Jesus one that attracted us to it and to Christ. At the first of many meetings Dallas had with my church staff over the years, he surprised me by referring to the fact that he and I both had trucks to use in working our properties—his an old, beat-up red Ford and mine a brand new, shiny white Ford-150 extended cab that I had picked him up in. With a playful tone of mock dismay, he said, "I am sure that Jesus would not have a truck like Keith has."

I remember meeting up with him and Keith Matthews for dinner just before a session, and when I opened his room door after knocking was embarrassed to see him in his boxer briefs, socks and undershirt. "Can I go like this?" he joked to Keith and me.

One of the last Dallas-isms I remember came after I finally started to write what I had learned due to Dallas's repeated prompting to do so. When a writing contract fell into my lap, he said, "Just remember, Keith, you are just a donkey pulling the Jesus cart."

May we each take up the Jesus cart God has given us and pull it like Dallas did, in the rhythms of Jesus' easy and light obedience.

Keith Meyer is the author of *Whole Life Transformation* and *Spiritual Rhythms in Community* and pastor of Hope Covenant Church, St. Cloud, Minnesota.

THE REAL DEAL

Ruth Haley Barton

Recently someone asked me what was the scariest speaking engagement I could remember, and immediately I knew which one it was. It was a conference on spiritual formation at a large church in our area during the days when spiritual formation was a relatively new category among evangelical Christians. I was in the early stages of my own training and experience in spiritual formation as well, so the invitation to participate in this conference was fairly intriguing. Somewhere in the process of accepting the invitation, the conference organizer let me know they had also secured Dallas Willard as a main speaker, and we would each give two addresses alternately. As if it wasn't nerve-racking enough to share the platform with Dallas, they also thought it would be really cool if we each listened to the other's addresses and then offered extemporaneous responses!

I am not sure which was the most intimidating: knowing that this brilliant teacher and philosopher would be listening and responding to what I was saying, *or* sitting in the audience while he was speaking knowing I was supposed to give some sort of intelligent response right there on the spot. *Who does this?* I wondered.

All the intelligent people I knew approached opportunities to interact with Dallas by preparing a list of questions and then letting him carry the day with his dry wit, unassuming personality and customary brilliance.

UNFORGETTABLE, THAT'S WHAT HE WAS

It is hard to describe the sheer panic I felt as I anticipated this spontaneous dialogue throughout the conference, but it was too late to back out; there would be no way out but through. As I listened to Dallas's first stirring and deeply insightful presentation, I was acutely aware of my own average intelligence and wondered how I could bluff my way through the event, hiding the fact that I was completely out of my league. While trying to appear confident I cast about, trying to figure out what I could possibly add to the depth, breadth and sheer brilliance of Dallas's message. Why he was not giving *all four* of the main messages is still a mystery to me!

Finally, by God's grace, I landed on a plan that began with accepting the fact that I could not match Dallas's intelligence and depth. Obvious, I know, but an important starting place. Then I decided that I would speak in the only voice I had—that of a spiritual director offering practical ideas for how folks could engage in spiritual practices that would open them to the different aspects of the kingdom that Dallas was so eloquently describing. It was really all I *could* do, and by all accounts it went fine.

Truth is, I don't remember much about the conference—probably because I've repressed it! But what I do remember is how Dallas bade me farewell when it was all over. In inimitable Dallas fashion, he took both of my hands in his, looked me straight in the eyes and with great kindness affirmed and thanked me for my contribution to the conference. I hadn't been spoken to with that much kindness for a long time and it's all I remember about that day. That this brilliant person, who could have rested on his laurels all day long, took time to offer sincere encouragement to a frightened, fledgling speaker was all the evidence I needed that this spiritual formation stuff really works.

WHAT I LEARNED FROM DALLAS

The trouble with being right. One of my favorite Dallas-isms is "It's hard to be right and not hurt anyone with it."[1] One can only guess that Dallas learned this lesson the hard way, and it struck me as one of the truest things I had ever heard! At first I applied it (a bit self-righteously) to every smart, well-educated, opinionated person I knew who seemed to wound people in their zeal for being right. But eventually I had to look in the mirror and admit, "I resemble that!" I had to acknowledge that even though I don't typically slice and dice people with my rightness, I do relish being right and when my rightness gets challenged I have been known to withdraw and withhold myself from those who do not share my views. I was grieved to admit that I have my own ways of being right and hurting others with it.

The good news is that his statement drew me into that godly grief that leads to repentance and it continually calls me to deeper levels of transformation every time I speak, write or try to communicate my ideas to others. I don't ask "What would Dallas say?" because no one will ever bring what he brought in terms of content. But I do sometimes ask "How would Dallas say it?" and that always changes me for the better. I am reminded of Paul's encouragement to his dear ones to "Keep on doing the things that you have learned and received and heard and seen in me, and the God of peace will be with you" (Phil 4:9 NRSV), and his exhortation that they would imitate him as he imitates Christ. I imagine that Dallas would have wanted the same for us.

Beyond false dichotomies. Another of Dallas's great contributions to my life and work is the natural way in which his perspective often dismantled false dichotomies that exist in human thought patterns. Early on in the spiritual formation movement many of us who were involved in seeker model churches and ministries were concerned that placing more emphasis on formation and discipleship would take the edge off people's evangelistic zeal. There was an understandable concern that such an emphasis would produce inwardly focused individuals who sat around gazing at their navels while the world went to hell in a hand basket. (An oversimplification, but you know what I'm trying to say.)

I spent a lot of words and huge amounts of energy trying to offer assurance and even inspiration that true transformation leads people to actually be *more* passionate and *more* effective in their evangelistic efforts, but to no avail. Dallas, on the other hand, had a way of saying things that immediately clarified large and complicated ideas, bringing such depth of wisdom and truth that no one even thought to argue. Almost effortlessly, he connected the dots between spiritual formation and evangelism.

> When the identified people of Christ reach a certain level of growth and don't go on, they limit their evangelistic potential. Why? Because the witness of the identified people of Christ to the reality of God in their own lives is weak and becomes a testimony to the contrary. To have earthshaking evangelism—you have to have a different quality of persons and that is what spiritual formation is all about.[2]

Dallas's articulation of this truth deepened my confidence that evangelism and spiritual formation are not mutually exclusive but are equally important aspects of the spiritual life that must be held together in creative tension if we are to live fruitful and balanced Christian lives. It so crystallized my thinking that when I was asked to speak at an evangelism conference, I pulled my thoughts together under the title *Evangelism: Invitation to Spiritual Transformation*, and I have loved communicating about evangelism in that way ever since.

While it is impossible to summarize the impact Dallas's life and ministry has had and will continue to have, if I were to try I would simply paraphrase Jack Nicholson's comment to Helen Hunt in the movie *As Good as It Gets*. After a lifetime of meanness, self-centeredness and egocentricity, Jack Nicholson's character experiences transformation in relationship with someone whose very presence brought out something better in him. To sum up the influence she had on his life he says, "You make me want to be a better man."

That's exactly how I felt around Dallas: he made me want to be a better person, and in fact he still does! May his life and witness continue to call out the best—the character of Christ—in all of us.

Ruth Haley Barton is founding president of The Transforming Center, a spiritual formation ministry to pastors and Christian leaders. Her most recent book is *Pursuing God's Will Together*.

EQUALLY AT HOME IN PRIVATE AND PUBLIC SPHERES

James Catford

Wednesday, May 26, 2010. The last day of what turned out to be the final visit Dallas Willard made to Britain was clear, bright and warm. As we sometimes did at the end of a busy speaking tour for Dallas, I arranged a special treat for him.

I booked for us places on one of those tour vehicles that run around the sights of big cities with a cheerful guide and lots of trivia about the people who once inhabited the city. Dallas joined the rest of our party as we waved at Buckingham Palace (just in case the Queen was looking out) and pointed to Nelson's Column. We had fun.

Halfway through the trip, to the delight of everyone on board, we waited at the top of a ramp right next to the iconic MI5 building, famous for James Bond 007, the fictitious British agent. With a nod and a wink our road driver swiftly left the vehicle and was replaced by a river pilot. Our vehicle edged its way forward and, with full throttle, shot down the beach and splashed straight into the river Thames.

We were in an amphibious Duck Tour landing craft, originally used in the Second World War, that went in a moment from land to water. Slowly we chugged downstream past the Houses of Parliament and eventually returned to our base beside the now famous London Eye. We posed and took pictures, not knowing that Dallas was saying goodbye to a culturally rich city that he loved.[1]

For me Dallas will always be an amphibious vehicle—someone whose remarkable mind could cruise around in the contemporary world like the rest of us and then, suddenly, plunge into the deep water of the Spirit. Like the bulky, bold vehicle in which we sat, the weight of Christ's presence within Dallas turned people in his direction whenever he was around. Why was this? It is because Dallas was equally at home in the church and the culture, the Bible and the world, heaven and earth. He was able to comfortably live in both contexts as if they are one. Why? Because they are one, or can be if approached in the right way.

This chapter explores a question that Dallas himself often considered: is it possible to navigate your way through this world without sacrificing a deep, personal and abiding relationship with God?

LONDON CALLING

I think Dallas enjoyed London because of the close proximity of church and state, commerce and Parliament, cathedrals and theaters. All were bunched up together in the same space. Once I took Dallas to meet the Archbishop of Canterbury at the time, George Carey. We then walked across Lambeth Bridge and into the majestic Palace of Westminster, home of the British Parliament, and later a presenter friend showed us around the BBC—all within a radius of a mile or so.

Everything being so close together gives London the quality of life lived in the moment. For the follower of Christ there really is no place to hide. The rich cultural and ethnic diversity of the place gives little cover for the person wanting to keep their faith in the shadows. With low church attendance, believers have little choice but to stand out in the crowd.

In Britain, if your workplace doesn't challenge what you believe then the media certainly will. This is the home of Richard Dawkins, the late Christopher Hitchens and all the rest of the liberal metropolitan elite. A great cultural conversation is taking place in the United Kingdom all the time, spilling out across movies, contemporary music, chat shows and mass circulation newspapers. Yet Dallas seemed to thrive here, willing to talk with any who cared to listen and happy to go to where the debate was taking place, outside the confines of the church and in the public square.

To understand why Dallas was so at home in this context, we have to grasp something of his theology of culture. He wrote:

> Jesus' good news about the kingdom can be an effective guide for our lives only if we share his view of the world in which we live. To his eyes this is a God-bathed and God-permeated world. It is a world filled with a glorious reality, where every component is within the range of God's direct knowledge and control—though he obviously permits some of it, for good reason, to be for a while otherwise than as he wishes. It is a world that is inconceivably beautiful and good because of God and because God is always in it. It is a world in which God is continually at play and over which he constantly rejoices. Until our thoughts of God have found every visible thing and event glorious with his presence, the word of Jesus has not yet fully seized us.[2]

Chapter three of *The Divine Conspiracy* sets out Dallas's foundations for a robust and radical theology of the material universe. He explains that "it is precisely from the space immediately around us that God watches and God acts." And "to be born 'from above,' in New Testament language, means to be interactively joined with a dynamic, unseen system of divine reality in the midst of which all of humanity moves about—whether it knows it or not."[3]

Dallas presses his point when he says that "heaven is here and God is here, because God and his spiritual agents act here and are constantly available here."[4] "Traveling through space and not finding God does not mean that space is empty any more than traveling through my body and not finding me means that I am not here."[5]

SEPARATING FAITH AND KNOWLEDGE: DEAL OR NO DEAL?

What is so arresting in what Dallas is saying is the way he confidently confronts the deal that seems to have been struck between the contemporary church and the prevailing worldview of our day.

It goes like this: keep religion in your heart if you must, but don't mix it up with life in the "real" world. Theologian N. T. Wright comments, "It is ironic that many people in the modern world have regarded Christianity as a private worldview, a set of private stories. Some Christians have actually played right into this trap. But in principle, the whole point of Christianity is that it offers a story which is the story of the whole world. It is public truth. Otherwise, it collapses into some version of Gnosticism."[6] (Gnosticism is a heresy that, in this context, idealizes inner knowledge as an exclusive form of salvation.)

Some philosophers like Stephen Jay Gould claim that there is "no overlapping magisterium" between personal religion and public reality. They simply don't mix. Dismissively, secularists sometimes insist that the best deal on the table for people of faith is to keep their faith personal. They think we should be grateful that they tolerate us at all.

Understanding this "deal" for what it is, Dallas responds that God "'in my heart' easily becomes 'in my imagination.' . . . If he is not in space at all, he is not in human life, which is lived in space."[7] Over breakfast with some business leaders in London, Dallas parodied a line taken by some believers that "you can't attack my religion because it's personal." This is only possible if and when faith and knowledge are seen as two different things. "Religion is never only personal, it is always public," Dallas would tell me.

Offered this choice of deal or no deal, Dallas would have none of it. He confidently took this view in his chosen academic field of philosophy, and especially phenomenology, and became a recognized world-class master at his profession. However, he readily understood that "the idea of an all-encompassing, all-penetrating world of God, interactive at every point with our lives, where we can always be totally at home and safe regardless of what happens in the visible dimension of the universe, is routinely treated as ridiculous."[8]

This attempt at a deal between what is patronizingly called the "faith community" and the prevailing culture has been hotly debated in Britain over the last couple of decades. The newspaper columnist Nick Cohen, writing in the *Observer* about the origins of life, is typical of this widely accepted view. "Today," he wrote, "you have to be a very ignorant believer to imagine that your religion or any religion can provide comprehensive explanations." He went on, "The most brilliant scientists and the best thought has moved beyond religion."[9]

Like a protective ozone layer, the covering of the church over the United States is now seriously breaking down. First it was the Bay Area, then the Pacific Northwest, then New England. If church attendance indicates anything, then the large cities of North America are becoming as de-churched as they are in Western Europe. It is likely that our model for "being church" is going to increasingly be of the exile rather than of the nation state. We'd better get ready.[10]

What makes Dallas's teaching of such lasting value is that it anticipates these shifting cultural patterns and firmly places a substantial intellectual anchor into the bedrock of reality that is more than capable of withstanding the cultural storms that are building. It is a teaching that makes no distinction between a language for the church and a language for the culture. Both have to navigate the same real world, a world that Dallas refused to be bullied into giving up to scientists, philosophers or any other gatekeepers of the public conversation.

Interacting with God and his kingdom is not a matter of "faith" but of knowledge. Like the people of God in exile, we have reached the point where we cannot compromise any longer. As Darrell Bock has so helpfully pointed out, in the cultural context of today the conflict around true Christianity concerns what is real. Dallas knew this and would not tolerate the category mistake of putting faith in Christ into the box of private opinion.[11]

ONE KINGDOM, FOUR SPACES

Whether it is an oversight of his editors or a deliberate move on Dallas's part, in his books *The Divine Conspiracy* and *Knowing Christ Today*[12] he repeats the same excerpt from the classic of English literature by Evelyn Waugh, *Brideshead Revisited*. In both places he uses the same extract to illustrate how the intellectual tide has gone out on much of what we call Christianity.

The passage Dallas selects to carry his argument is one where the character Charles Ryder says, "The view implicit in my education was that the basic narrative of Christianity had long been exposed as a myth." In the context of the public square, what Dallas found sobering was Ryder's claim that "no one had ever suggested to me that these quaint observations expressed a coherent philosophical system and intransigent historical claims; nor, had they done so, would I have been much interested."[13]

It's as if this example of a view widely held today is a bridge between Dallas's two key books of Christian scholarship and learning. While *The Divine Conspiracy* sets out a foundational view of "a God-bathed world," *Knowing Christ Today* extends this teaching right into the public square. Dallas takes the groundwork of his earlier thinking and applies it more extensively to a range of settings including apologetics, the disappearance of moral knowledge and the place of the church in the world.

It is likely that this later work will be less widely read than his earlier teaching, but to understand Dallas we need to see them as parts of a whole. Dallas realized that getting the church into a meaningful conversation about culture is hard because the church is so reluctant to open a conversation with the world on an equal footing. First convert the church, was often his cry.

Now, of course, the culture has also become more wary of engaging in conversation with the church. But as Dallas sometimes pointed out, if the gatekeepers and opinion formers of society could see that the Bible had very much to offer for living life well, then they wouldn't treat it with the disdain that they so often do.

Dallas lived as he taught that to privatize the kingdom to the confines of the church is only one step better than hiding it deep within our hearts. In saying this he stands with many other writers and leaders of the church—N. T. Wright, John Stott and Pope Benedict to name but a few. And yet, outside this notable group the pull of our leaders is less toward a courageous engagement with the world than it is to a deeper life with Christ. Yet both—and combined—are essential for Christ and his kingdom to be seen bursting forth in our day.

Through Dallas I have come to understand that we all live in four spaces, and all at the same time.

RECLAIMING PRIVATE SPACE

There is private space, which can be defined by answering the question, *Who are you when no one is looking?* Here we exist at the most profound level. In my own conversations with Dallas he would often advise me to have more silence, more solitude. As he observed me at close quarters he encouraged me to live a more considered and reflective life. I will always be grateful for him telling me that he trained himself to wake up each morning praying and looking over the forthcoming day, releasing control over it, one task or encounter at a time.

Now both silence and solitude have become fused into me and shape much of the rhythm of my life. At one time as a young man hooked on contemporary music, I found it impossible to drive my car without the radio on, and turned up loud. That may never have been your problem, but noise of one kind or another is the number-one enemy of intimacy with God. Silence has now become my friend, and I crave it like a duck craves water.

Reclaiming Intimate Space

The second space we inhabit is intimate space, which we can define as *I can't do this for just anybody, but I can do it for you.* By this I mean there is a small set of people with whom we are most intimate, such as our spouse if we have one, our closest family and our friends. These are the people we share our life with, and the ones who know us best.

There were the twelve disciples—the people, as Dallas liked to say, that Jesus took on a three-year camping trip. Chosen carefully, our closest "formation friends" are the people around us who love us further into the kingdom. The ones with whom we can be the most vulnerable as we face up to our humanity, our shame and our need for forgiveness.

Prompted by the teaching Dallas gave on the historic disciplines of the Christian life, I once spent a week on the San Juan Islands with a mutual friend, Lutheran pastor Bill Vaswig. There I entered into the discipline of confession as I stayed up late one evening writing page after page about my life from childhood through to middle age. The next morning, determined not to undercook the exercise and need to do it all over again, I made my confession to Bill. It changed my life more than I can say.

Such times of confession can be rich and liberating. We need a wise and trusted friend to help us and to be totally confidential with what they hear. But it doesn't take a remote island or a week of your life to experience the freedom of releasing your failings in this way.

If your church teaches that this practice is to be done with an ordained leader, then that is the route to go—but still go.

RECLAIMING SOCIAL SPACE

The third space in which we live is the social space, or the people to whom we say, *I recognize you*. These are the people in our address book and who might expect a Christmas card from us, colleagues at work, people at the gym or even people at church.

It is in social space that we can make the most impact in the world. Dallas was keen to live fully in this space himself, whether at his own workplace or among the many people who, like me, looked to him for spiritual support and occasional guidance. I most appreciated his gentle touch on the hand or the knee, his willingness to walk and talk through the streets of London, and his complete openness to discuss any subject from human sexuality to the miracles of Jesus.

Often our engagement with social space is about doing what we are already doing, but just better or more intentionally. Sometimes we don't even recognize the touch points we have with our local community, workplace, college or sports club; we can start by doing a simple review of how we spend our time and who we come in contact with. This is a matter of prayer as we audit our lives in this and all the spaces.

RECLAIMING PUBLIC SPACE

The final space in which we live is public space, or what we could call *life out there*. Here the emphasis is on the public square and the world with which we have little or no direct connection unless we deliberately choose to do so. This could include national politics, world poverty, the media and the movies.

Dallas once spent a week with the Bible Society that I lead, visiting our offices in Swindon and London. He took a great interest in the four drivers of our culture that the Bible Society has identified as *media, government,* the *arts* and *education.* Later he took part in a public debate at a prestigious arts venue in central London hosted by the think tank Theos.

Chaired by a well-known commentator and journalist, the debate's topic was "How much religious liberty can a liberal society afford?" Dallas sat comfortably alongside a leading Muslim, a leading humanist and a leading philosopher of religion. He contributed to the debate not just by his insightful comments, but by the sheer weight of his gracious presence.

I found that watching how Dallas handled these kinds of situations helped me to become a better apprentice of Jesus Christ. We all need people who show us in very practical terms how to live out a deep, personal and abiding relationship with Christ. During my life I have always sought out people who appear to do life better than I do and to learn from them.

In doing this we will be sure to start small and to gradually learn how to conduct ourselves in the public eye. This could be the corporate world of business or academia, or out there in civic life. It doesn't happen overnight and we can expect to make mistakes. But, as Dallas would also say, life is supposed to be interesting, and there's little doubt that it will be if we take it seriously in the public square.

What impressed me over the time that I knew Dallas was the way he moved so freely among these four spaces. Like an amphibious vehicle, he was equally at home in all environments, all weathers and all spaces.

COACHING THE NATIONS

Dallas would have liked to have written more on the public square. The last chapter of *Knowing Christ Today* gives a glimpse of what he had in mind. His concern was to see pastors as teachers of the nations, and he opened the chapter by asking, "Who is to bring the knowledge that will answer the great life questions that perplex humanity?"[14]

He firmly believed that the Christian church is a public institution, "a familiar social reality" that continues to have a "massive
public presence in the world."[15] In this context, "pastors for Christ
teach the 'nations' by declaring the presence of the kingdom everywhere and by pointing out the availability of eternal life now in the
kingdom of God." Dallas loved to say that "discipleship is for the
sake of the world."[16]

Dallas sets out a vision for pastors to "guide disciples into their
place in their world and show them how to 'exercise dominion in
life through one man, Christ Jesus' (Rom. 5:17)."[17] This applies as
much to working in IT or banking as it does to the laboratory, farm,
schoolroom, media, sports, fine arts, government and the academy.
Church, for Dallas, is to be a school of love. We are to coach the
nations in how to live well, to coach them for Christ.

Sitting in the rear of a car in south London on our way back from
a speaking engagement, Dallas leaned forward to catch the attention of my wife, Sue, and myself. We had been talking for several
days about the rise of the new atheism, the sidelining of the church
in contemporary culture and the loss of confidence that many
Christians have in their own text, the Bible.

In the way that Dallas so often delivered the killer line in a conversation, he brought the whole matter together in one statement:
"Don't worry about secularism," he said, "let secularism worry about
you." He went on to say that "it can never deal adequately with the
fine texture of life." This is both the challenge and the opportunity
that Dallas left for us.

It felt like we had just run down the bank of the Thames and hit
the water.

Dallas took his understanding of the kingdom of God and confidently rowed it out onto the deep water of secular society. He
seemed fearless in the face of opposition and knew exactly how to
detonate powerful questions that would change a conversation in
an instant. For us not to worry about secularism, we will need to

pursue the deeper life with God that Dallas has become so famous for. Essentially this is in the private and intimate spaces.

However, Dallas was equally at home in the social space of his workplace and the public space of national life. We may be a blue- or white-collar worker but we can still make an impact for Jesus right where we have been placed by him. Finding out what that means for us is what makes life so interesting.

His amphibious nature enabled Dallas to move effortlessly between life with God and life in the world. He modeled how to swim against even the strongest currents, and he called the church to return to its mission of coaching all nations to lead life well through the person and work of Jesus Christ. Can you navigate your way through this world without compromising a deeper life with God? For Dallas the answer was unmistakably *yes*. Now it's our turn to show how it's done.

James Catford is group chief executive of Bible Society (BFBS, England and Wales) and a former publishing director at HodderHeadline and HarperCollins. He is a former vice-chair of Renovaré and is chair of Renovaré Britain and Ireland.

20

CONCLUSION: HEY DALLAS . . .

John Ortberg

When Dallas woke up, he would begin his day with either Psalm 23 or the Lord's Prayer. His own version of the latter was unforgettable, and well worth living in for a moment now—for even in the midst of paper and dots of ink, Jesus is present.

Dear Father always near us,
May your name be treasured and loved,
May your rule be completed in us—May your will be done
    here on earth
in just the way it is done in heaven.
Give us today the things we need today,
And forgive us our sins and impositions on you as we are
    forgiving all who in any way offend us.
Please don't put us through trials, but deliver us from
    everything bad.
Because you are the one in charge, and you have all the
    power, and the glory too is all yours—forever—
    Which is just the way we want it!

Dallas used to say that "Which is just the way we want it" is a good way to translate "Amen." Or, he said, sometimes if your nerves can stand it, you might just try saying, "Whoopee."

Someday, when I see him again, I think that's the word I'll use.

Somebody asked Dallas once, "Hey Dallas, do you believe in total depravity?" And Dallas said, "I believe in *sufficient* depravity." This is so Dallas. He would say things nobody else could say, and there would be this response, this rolling laughter, and then deep thought.

"I believe in sufficient depravity."

"What is that?"

"I believe everyone is sufficiently depraved that when we get to heaven no one will be able to say 'I merited this.'"

The doctrine of sufficient depravity is one of a thousand doctrines from Dallas that seems as if we'd never heard it before, and yet the more you think about it seems as if it always must have been. One of the strange mental pictures that I've had since his passing is of Dallas going to the pearly gates and then being sent back to earth with a stamp marked "Insufficient depravity—Requires a little more dissipation to make sure atonement was really needed." However, it is important to remember that Dallas too was sufficiently depraved.

Dallas did not want to be made much of at his memorial service, but we could not help violating that at least a little. Gary Black said to Dallas, "At that memorial your will will no longer be reigning." But it's true that to truly honor Dallas, we must not over-honor Dallas. Or to put it another way, what we love above all is Jesus. What we love best in Dallas is the Jesus in him. And we honor Dallas most when we look through and beyond him to the One to whom Dallas constantly and joyfully and unstoppably and promiscuously pointed. Because to me the best moments, the moments I will miss most, are when there was no hurry, no schedule constraint, nothing at all in the world but time, God and love, and you could just ask, "Hey Dallas . . ."

How many stories about him begin, "Somebody asked Dallas . . ."
"Hey Dallas . . ."

And you could see him thinking. Not about the problem, which he had worked out long ago, but about how to express it in a way that those of us listening to him might be able to grasp what he was saying and benefit from it, so that it would not become a pearl cast among swine—one of dozens of Scripture passages that I heard Dallas explain better than any professional exegete I ever knew—and so that it would cause us to love Jesus more than we could imagine.

"Hey Dallas, who is God?"

"God is the happiest, most joyful being in the universe."

"Hey Dallas, who's going to heaven?"

"I'm quite sure that God will allow everyone into heaven that can possibly stand it."

"Hey Dallas, what's hell?"

"Hell is just the best God can do for some people."

He was ruthlessly committed to logic and clarity of thought, and the constant, uncompromising cultivation of reason. This is indispensable to navigating reality, and helping people navigate reality is indispensable to love.

"Hey Dallas, what is reality?"

"Reality is what you can count on."

"Hey Dallas, what is pain?"

"Pain is what you experience when you bump into reality."

And because of this, Dallas had a deep aversion to speakers, especially in the Christian community, who would try to use emotion to manipulate an inevitably temporary response from listeners that would then leave them worse off than before. Dallas once noted his belief that for this reason, speakers should never tell stories. After that Gary Moon and I decided that we would publish the Dallas Willard Study Bible with all the stories taken out. Which would leave pretty much just Leviticus. There is a wonderful story about what happened next, and I would tell you, but then I would be telling a story, and Dallas wouldn't like that, so I can't do that.

"Hey Dallas, what is spiritual maturity?"

"A mature disciple is the one who effortlessly does what Jesus would do in his or her place."

"Hey Dallas, what does it mean to glorify God?"

"To glorify God means to think and act in such a way that the goodness, greatness and beauty of God are constantly obvious to you and all those around you."

And this is true. Dallas glorified God. It was hard to look at Dallas and be around him and not think, "Thank God for God, if God could think up somebody like that."

It has been well over twenty years since I first read the book that would change my life, *The Spirit of the Disciplines*, and then contacted Dallas. To my surprise he invited me to their home. All I knew about him at that time was that he taught philosophy at USC and he wrote about spiritual disciplines. I imagined he was an East Coast, Ivy League, tweed-jacket, sherry-drinking, Episcopalian kind of guy. I was not prepared for how humble he was. I was not prepared for how at peace his body was. I was not prepared for how good he was. I was not prepared for that house.

He was the most amazing mind I had ever encountered, but his heart was so much better than his mind. And it was just in his body.

I got a copy of the talks that he did about the kingdom of God for a Sunday school class at Hollywood Presbyterian. We lived in Simi Valley then, well over twenty years ago, and I listened to that recording over and over. I remember Dallas saying at the beginning of that, as he laid out his assumptions, what simply made so much sense. One of his assumptions he stated was, "I assume that I am wrong about some things, because everybody else I know is wrong about some things, and it would be very unusual." And I have found myself over these last days wondering, what has Dallas found out he was wrong about?

I have this odd picture in my mind of Dallas going up to the pearly gates and God saying to him, "Hey Dallas, we actually *do* use a barcode scanner here!"

I remember a time I went to him with a more personal problem: "Hey Dallas, my heart is breaking, I can't fix it, I don't understand it, and I'm sadder than I've ever been in my life."

There was a long pause. With Dallas there's always a long pause. And then he said, "This will be a test of your joyful confidence in God."

I've thought about that sentence a thousand times.

I remember sitting at the table at that little house in Box Canyon many years ago in a real deep valley, and spending a day talking and praying with Dallas and Jane, and then Dallas put his hand over my heart to pray for me. Nobody had ever done that before. If you were with him, or you just read his words, you know that there's something coming through from someplace else.

Listening to Dallas think, listening to him talk, you could get lost with delight in the sheer joy of a master craftsman. Like watching Gene Kelly dance. Except that it was not about the craft. It was about the life and reality and goodness of the one who stood behind the thought and beyond the words.

One of the things Dallas said the last year he was walking through his illness was that he felt he had trusted too much in his own cleverness with words. And I thought it must have been hard to be so smart.

I will miss the tremor in his voice when he saw the wonder. I think that in some ways his presence, his life, was kind of like that wardrobe into Narnia, where it's not about the wardrobe, it's about a luminous world beyond the wardrobe that the wardrobe is the door to. But you love the wardrobe still.

"Hey Dallas, what's death?"

"Jesus made a point of saying that only those who rely on him and have received the kind of life that flows in him and in God will never experience death. Jesus shows his apprentices how to live in light of the fact that they will never stop living."

There's a passage, and in particular one line, from John 16 that I thought about a lot over the weeks surrounding Dallas's death. Jesus is going to die, and he's talking to his little band of followers and friends.

> "In a little while you will see me no more, and then after a little while you will see me."
>
> At this, some of his disciples said to one another, "What does he mean by saying, 'In a little while you will see me no more, and then after a little while you will see me,' and 'Because I am going to the Father'?" They kept asking, "What does he mean by 'a little while'? We don't understand what he is saying."
>
> Jesus saw that they wanted to ask him about this, so he said to them, "Are you asking one another what I meant when I said, 'In a little while you will see me no more, and then after a little while you will see me'?" (Jn 16:16-19 NIV)

Does that sound a little like Dallas and his friends? John is kind of drawing out the opaqueness here. And then Jesus says,

> "You will grieve, but your grief will turn to joy. A woman giving birth to a child has pain because her time has come; but when her baby is born she forgets the anguish because of her joy that a child is born into the world. So with you: Now is your time of grief, but I will see you again and you will rejoice, and no one will take away your joy. In that day you will no longer ask me anything." (Jn 16:20-23 NIV)

I was thinking about how the disciples were forever pestering Jesus with questions. "Hey Jesus, can I sit at your right hand when I die?" "Hey Jesus, how many times do I have to forgive this guy?" "Hey Jesus, why was this man born blind?" "Hey Jesus, what's this parable mean?" "Hey Jesus, should we bring fire down on the Samaritans?" "Hey Jesus, who's the greatest?" "Hey Jesus, how long? How long before the kingdom? How long?"

When our first child was born, I was—we were—unprepared for the barrage of unanswerable questions that would come from her. Just constant, nonstop, impossible to answer. And one day in the car, when she was maybe two or three years old, I suddenly had this odd idea. I turned the tables and started asking her, "Hey Laura, why does the grass grow? Hey Laura, why is the sky blue? Hey Laura, why does the sun shine? Hey Laura, what makes the car go?"

And she got this real confused look on her face, and her lower lip started trembling, and Nancy, who had to live with these questions every day, got really happy and said, "Keep going, John! Make her cry! Make her cry!"

I wonder sometimes if Dallas ever got tired of all the questions: I wonder sometimes if Jesus ever got tired of all the questions. And underneath them all is the great question, *Why?*

Why is there cancer? Why are there tears? Why did Dallas have to die? Why can't he be with us so we could see him?

And the one we love says to us still, "For a little while I will be gone, and you will see terrible things." Cancer and pain and suffering and loss and death. "And then in a little while—it will seem like a long time for you, but it's just a little while—I am coming back." And then this promise that I had not noticed before, "On that day you will ask me no more questions."

Another very wise man said a long time ago, "For it is the nature of joy that all questions grow silent and nothing needs explaining." It's the nature of joy.

"Hey Dallas, what's joy?"

"A pervasive and constant unending sense of well-being."

On that day we will see our friend, and there will be no more questions. Because we'll just see. We'll all just see. Because we'll know, not just in our thoughts but in our bodies. And it will be just a little while, only a little while. In between then and now we miss him and love him, as we do all those we have loved and lost.

But another day is coming.

Whoopee.

Notes

Preface

[1]From a personal conversation with Gary Black a few minutes after Dallas died. Gary was with Dallas at his passing.

[2]Aaron Preston is a former undergraduate and PhD student under Dallas Willard. He is currently an associate professor of philosophy and chair of the philosophy department at Valparaiso University.

[3]From Scott Soames's opening remarks at the USC memorial service for Dallas Willard, October 4, 2013.

[4]Dallas Willard's primary influence was on evangelical Protestant churches.

[5]Joe Gorra, "Dallas Willard (1935–2013): Life-long Learner and Lover of Christ Jesus and His Kingdom," EPS blog, May 8, 2013, http://blog .epsociety.org/2013/05/dallas-willard-1935-2013-life-long.html.

[6]Aaron Preston, "Dallas Willard: My Beloved Rabboni," www.epsociety.org /library/articles.asp?pid=178

Introduction

[1]City of Buffalo, "Area History," www.buffalomissouri.us/about/area-history.

[2]I had the opportunity to interview Dallas Willard on several occasions in my role as director of the Dallas Willard Center in preparation for a life story project. Unless otherwise noted, extended quotations are from Dallas Willard and taken from the transcripts of those interviews.

[3]It is perhaps more precise to say that Albert Willard was a farmer on the side while his primary vocation was that of a county tax collector who served from time to time as the county treasurer.

[4]The title of Dallas Willard's PhD dissertation was "Meaning and Universals in Husserl's *Logische Untersuchungen*."

[5]Dallas avoided "officially" participating in a mentoring relationship with

another individual, preferring to simply do things together or be together.

[6]John Ortberg, "Dallas Willard, a Man from Another 'Time Zone,'" *Christianity Today*, May 8, 2013, www.christianitytoday.com/ct/2013/may-web -only/man-from-another-time-zone.html.

[7]See http://dallaswillardcenter.com/renovare-institute.

[8]Dallas Willard, *The Divine Conspiracy* (San Francisco: HarperCollins, 1998), p. xvii.

[9]See the section "The Evidential Force of Dallas Willard" in chapter six of this book.

The Funeral Service at Dallas's Home Church

[1]Dallas Willard's home church is Valley Vineyard Christian Fellowship of Reseda, California.

[2]The Tardis is a reference to the time-travel device used in the British television series *Doctor Who*. The structure appears larger and grander on the inside than on the outside.

[3]Words from a prayer Jane Willard read at the service. It was often spoken by Dallas as a mealtime prayer.

[4]Knowing Christ Today Conference, February 2013, Santa Barbara, California.

Chapter 1: If Death My Friend and Me Divide

[1]C. S. Lewis, *The Last Battle* (1956; New York: HarperCollins, 2000), pp. 210-11.

Chapter 2: Family Voices

[1]In Dallas Willard, *Renovation of the Heart* (Colorado Springs: NavPress, 2002), p. 100.

[2]This phrase was likely first recorded in Dallas Willard, "Your Place in This World," commencement address, Greenville College, May 2004, www .dwillard.org/articles/artview.asp?artid=109.

Chapter 3: A Word from a Different Reality

[1]Dallas Willard, *The Divine Conspiracy* (San Francisco: HarperCollins, 1998), p. 11.

[2]*American Heritage Dictionary*, 2nd college ed., s.v. "sarcasm"; and W. E. Vine, Merrill F. Unger and William White, *Vine's Expository Dictionary of Biblical Words* (Nashville, TN: Thomas Nelson Publishers, 1985), pp. 242, 286.

[3]Willard, *Divine Conspiracy*, p. 151.

[4]Willard, *Divine Conspiracy*, pp. 305, 316, 372.

[5]Jan Johnson, "Apprentice to the Master," *Discipleship Journal* 107 (September/October 1998): 26.

[6]Dallas Willard, *Renovation of the Heart* (Colorado Springs: NavPress, 2002), p. 209.

THE USC SERVICE

[1]The comment was made by a student and friend of Dallas Willard, Ara Astourian.

[2]Dallas Willard, "Can Wisdom Be Taught?" *Roundtable*, 1971, www.dwillard.org/articles/artview.asp?artID=168.

CHAPTER 5: THE EVIDENTIAL FORCE OF DALLAS WILLARD

[1]Dallas makes this point evident throughout his body of writings. I attempt to provide a terse summary of Dallas's book-length writings on spiritual formation in my "The Willardian Corpus," *The Journal of Spiritual Formation and Soul Care* 3:2 (2010): 239-66. For this point in particular, see pp. 248-51.

[2]Dallas Willard, "Spiritual Formation and the Warfare Between the Flesh and Human Spirit," *The Journal of Spiritual Formation and Soul Care* 1:1 (2008): 86.

[3]Dallas Willard, *The Spirit of the Disciplines: Understanding How God Changes Lives* (New York: HarperCollins, 1988), p. ix.

[4]Ibid, p. xi.

[5]Ibid, p. 120.

[6]See, for instance, Dallas Willard, *Knowing Christ Today: Why We Can Trust Spiritual Knowledge* (New York: HarperCollins, 2009), p. 161.

[7]See Philip Yancey's introduction to G. K. Chesterton's *Orthodoxy* (New York: Image, 1991).

[8]Sheldon Vanauken, *A Severe Mercy* (New York: Harper & Row, 1977), p. 85.

[9]Dallas Willard, "When God Moves In," in *Indelible Ink*, ed. Scott Larsen (Colorado Springs: WaterBrook, 2003), p. 51-52.

[10]Dallas Willard, "The Three-Stage Argument for the Existence of God," in *Contemporary Perspectives on Religious Epistemology*, ed. R. Douglas Geivett and Brendan Sweetman (Oxford: Oxford University Press, 1992), p. 223-24.

[11]Willard, *Spirit of the Disciplines*, p. 243-44.

**CHAPTER 6: MOVING BEYOND THE CORNER OF THE
CHECKERBOARD**

[1]Os Guinness, *Long Journey Home: A Guide to Your Search for the Meaning of Life* (Colorado Springs: WaterBrook, 2001), p. 12.

[2]What is not easy to see is how research is possible without truth or knowledge. Of course, this could be a potential field of research!

[3]The details of this complex issue are beyond the scope of this chapter. See Greg Jesson, "The Impossibility of Philosophical Skepticism," in *Defending Realism: Ontological and Epistemological Investigations*, ed. Guido Bonino, Greg Jesson and Javier Cumpa Arteseros (Berlin: de Gruyter Press, 2014).

[4]Dallas's translation; *Knowing Christ Today: Why We Can Trust Spiritual Knowledge* (New York: HarperCollins, 2009), chap. 2.

[5]Another, and more exact, way to state this position is that none of these facts are constituted by being perceived or thought of.

[6]Dallas Willard, *Knowing Christ Today*, p. 44.

[7]If one is not claiming that his or her view is true, or if one is claiming not to know the view he or she is defending, then the whole position collapses into self-contradiction. To say "Today is Tuesday but I am not saying that this is true," or "401 is a prime number, but I am not saying that this is true," is as confused and muddled as any view can possibly be. Similarly, to deny that one has vast amounts of knowledge is equally self-defeating and absurd. Imagine your physician, dentist, contractor, student or car mechanic announcing that he or she does not know anything, not even that he or she knows that!

[8]Richard Rorty was one of the most controversial philosophers of the last half century, saying things such as, "Truth is merely what you let your friends get away with." His ideas were pivotal in promoting so-called postmodern thought, which paradoxically rejects the ideas of truth, evidence, reason and knowledge.

[9]See H. A. Prichard, "The History of the Theory of Knowledge," in *Knowledge and Perception* (Oxford: Oxford University Press, 1970).

[10]More will be said about intentionality later; briefly, it is a unique feature of mental states, such as thoughts and perceptions, wherein each mental state "points" or directs our attention to something other than itself. If someone asks you what you are thinking about, you can tell them the

"object" to which your thought is pointing—even if it is something confused and hazy. Jean-Paul Sartre called this feature of consciousness "a mystery in broad daylight," because it is present in every conscious moment of our lives, but when one tries to explain how it works, things get complicated.

[11] See C. S. Lewis, "The Poison of Subjectivism," in *Christian Reflections*, ed. Walter Hooper (Grand Rapids: Eerdmans, 1967), p. 72.

[12] G. E. Moore, "The Refutation of Idealism," in *Philosophical Studies* (New York: Harcourt, Brace & Co., 1922), p. 27; he says, "There is, therefore, no question of how we are to 'get outside the circle of our ideas and sensations.' Merely to have a sensation is already to *be* outside that circle."

[13] See Laird Addis, *Natural Signs: A Theory of Intentionality* (Philadelphia: Temple University Press, 1989), chap. one.

[14] Aristotle, *Metaphysics*, 993b.9-10.

[15] I have written a much more detailed account of the issues raised here, which was published as "The Husserlian Roots of Dallas Willard's Philosophical and Religious Works: Knowledge of the Temporal and the Eternal," in *Philosophia Christi*, Summer 2014.

CHAPTER 7: FROM SECULAR PHILOSOPHY TO FAITH

[1] I also took Dallas's courses on "History of Ethics to 1900" and "History of Western Philosophy: Modern Period."

[2] Dallas Willard, "The Redemption of Reason" (address, Biola University's Academic Symposium on "The Christian University in the Next Millennium," La Mirada, CA, February 28, 1998), www.dwillard.org/articles/artview.asp?artID=118.

[3] Ibid.

[4] Ibid.

[5] Dallas Willard, *The Divine Conspiracy* (San Francisco: HarperCollins, 1998), p. 194.

[6] Dallas Willard, "Who Is Your Teacher?" in *The Great Omission: Reclaiming Jesus's Essential Teachings on Discipleship* (San Francisco: HarperCollins, 2006), pp. 18-22, especially 20.

[7] Dallas Willard, *Renovation of the Heart: Putting on the Character of Christ* (Colorado Springs: NavPress, 2002), pp. 41-42, 85; Dallas Willard, *The Spirit of the Disciplines: Understanding How God Changes Lives* (New York: HarperCollins, 1999), p. ix.

[8]Athanasius, "Letters to Serapion," in *Works on the Spirit: Athanasius the Great and Didymus the Blind*, trans. Mark DelCogliano, Andrew Radde-Gallwitz and Lewis Ayres (Yonkers, NY: St. Vladimir's Seminary Press, 2011), pp. 88-91; David Brakke, *Athanasius and the Politics of Asceticism* (New York: Oxford University Press, 1995), pp. 142-200, especially 149, 167.

[9]St. Basil the Great, *On the Holy Spirit*, trans. Stephen Hildebrand (Yonkers, NY: St. Vladimir's Seminary Press, 2011), pp. 54, 66-67, 85-86.

[10]For a concise and very helpful point of entry to early Christian discussion of salvation as participation in divine life, see J. A. McGuckin, "Deification in Greek Patristic Thought: The Cappadocian Fathers' Strategic Adaptation of a Tradition," in Michael Christensen and Jeffery Wittung, eds., *Partakers of the Divine Nature: The History and Development of Deification in the Christian Traditions* (Madison, NJ: Fairleigh Dickinson University Press, 2006).

[11]Stephen Thomas, "Deification," in *The Encyclopedia of Eastern Orthodox Christianity*, ed. J. A. McGuckin (Chichester, UK: Wiley-Blackwell, 2011), p. 183.

[12]Archbishop Lazar Puhalo, *Freedom to Believe: Personhood and Freedom in Orthodox Christian Ontology*, 2nd ed. (Dewdney, BC: Synaxis Press, 2007), pp. 91-92.

[13]St. Symeon the New Theologian, *On the Mystical Life: The Ethical Discourses*, vol. 3, *Life, Times and Theology*, trans. Alexander Golitzin (Crestwood, NY: St. Vladimir's Seminary Press, 1997), pp. 39-40.

Chapter 8: Reflections on a Day with My Professor and Friend

[1]Dallas Willard, *The Divine Conspiracy* (San Francisco: HarperCollins, 1998), p. 92. See also pp. 75, 79, 134, 184-85.

[2]Dallas Willard, *Knowing Christ Today* (New York: HarperCollins, 2009).

[3]Dallas Willard, *Renovation of the Heart* (Colorado Springs: NavPress, 2002).

[4]See Dallas Willard, "How Concepts Relate the Mind to Its Objects: The 'God's Eye View' Vindicated," *Philosophia Christi* 1, no. 2 (Winter 1999): 5-20.

[5]Stanley Grenz, *Revisioning Evangelical Theology* (Downers Grove, IL: InterVarsity Press, 1993), p. 15.

[6]See J. P. Moreland, *Kingdom Triangle* (Grand Rapids: Zondervan, 2007), chapter 3.

[7]Willard, *Renovation of the Heart*, pp. 28-29, 43-44.

[8]For example, see Crystal McVea, *Waking Up in Heaven* (New York: Simon & Shuster, 2013), pp. 121-30. While this account is based on testimony, it must be remembered that psychologists do not have direct access to a patient's inner consciousness, and to know about that consciousness, psychologists must rely on first-person testimony.

[9]See J. P. Moreland, *The Soul: How We Know It's Real and Why It Matters* (Chicago: Moody Publishers, 2014).

CHAPTER 10: WIDENING SPHERES OF INFLUENCE

[1]Henri Nouwen, "Being the Beloved," sermon 1 of 8, www.youtube.com/watch?v=SFWfYpdoF18.

[2]Dallas Willard, 2009 Renovaré Institute Lecture.

[3]Ibid.

[4]Dallas Willard, *The Spirit of the Disciplines* (New York: HarperCollins, 1991), p. ix.

[5]Dallas Willard, *Renovation of the Heart* (Colorado Springs: NavPress, 2002), p. 98.

CHAPTER 12: JOURNEY INTO JOY

[1]Dallas Willard, *The Divine Conspiracy* (San Francisco: HarperCollins, 1998), p. 62.

[2]Personal correspondence, May 2, 1995.

[3]Dallas Willard, *The Spirit of the Disciplines* (San Francisco: HarperCollins, 1988), p. 179.

CHAPTER 13: DALLAS WILLARD, EVANGELIST

[1]Dallas Willard, *The Divine Conspiracy* (San Francisco: HarperCollins, 1998), p. xiii (emphasis mine).

[2]Ibid., p. 13.

[3]Ibid., p. 15.

[4]Ibid., p. 35.

[5]Ibid., p. 304.

[6]Ibid., p. 12.

[7]Ibid., p. 134.

[8]Ibid., p. 185.

[9]Ibid., p. 233.

[10]Ibid., p. 271.

[11]Ibid., p. 316.

[12]Ibid.

[13]Ibid., p. 2.

[14]Dallas Willard, *The Great Omission* (San Francisco: HarperCollins, 2006), p. 62.

[15]Willard, *Divine Conspiracy*, p. xvi.

[16]Ibid.

[17]This definition comes from a work group I participated in with Dallas Willard at a Theological and Cultural Thinkers (TACT) meeting, sponsored by Mission America. While several of us in the group may have contributed to the statement, Willard was the intellectual force behind the stunning picture it painted.

[18]Dallas Willard, *Knowing Christ Today* (New York: HarperCollins, 2009), p. 15.

[19]Ibid., p. 20.

[20]Ibid., p. 39.

[21]Ibid., p. 45.

[22]Ibid., p. 83.

[23]Willard, *Divine Conspiracy*, p. 48.

[24]Ibid., p. 49.

[25]Willard, *Knowing Christ Today*, p. 139 (emphasis his).

[26]Ibid., p. 142.

[27]Ibid., p. 146.

[28]Ibid., p. 147.

[29]Ibid., p. 153.

[30]Willard, *The Great Omission*, p. x (emphasis his).

[31]Willard, *Knowing Christ Today*, p. 156 (emphasis mine).

[32]Willard, *Divine Conspiracy*, p. 21.

CHAPTER 14: DEVELOPING PASTORS AND CHURCHES OF THE KINGDOM

[1]Involving six three-day retreats over two or three years with a community of twenty-five leaders, the Journey is The Leadership Institute's most extensive non-academic training. The Journey seeks to train leaders to follow Jesus' patterns of withdrawing from public ministry periodically to make space to commune with his Father and to rest. Jesus led his disciples into this way of life, which Scripture and current research show

fosters the deep personal and ministry transformation that God desires.

[2]Dallas shared this insight in a lecture titled "Developing a Theology and Models of the Church" at the Journey on May 5, 1998.

[3]Thomas Kelly, *A Testament of Devotion* (New York: Harper & Brothers, 1941), p. 36.

CHAPTER 15: *GRAY'S ANATOMY* AND THE SOUL

[1]Dallas Willard, *Renovation of the Heart* (Colorado Springs: NavPress, 2002), pp. 202-3.

[2]Ibid., p. 205.

CHAPTER 17: A FEW DALLAS-ISMS THAT CHANGED MY LIFE

[1]From a talk given at staff training, Church of the Open Door, August 15, 2004.

[2]TACT think tank meeting, September 21, 2002.

[3]TACT meeting, September 17, 2004.

[4]Meeting with Dallas and Oak Hills staff, November 7, 2004.

[5]Fuller Theological Seminary course, June 8, 2006.

[6]Adapted from John Henry Newman, "Jesus the Light of the Soul."

CHAPTER 18: THE REAL DEAL

[1]I first heard this quote from John Ortberg after he returned from a conference with Dallas Willard. It has since been documented in Ortberg, *God Is Closer than You Think* (Grand Rapids: Zondervan, 2005), p. 148.

[2]Dallas Willard, in response to a question about the connection between spiritual formation and evangelism, at a staff day at Willow Creek Community Church, April 1999.

CHAPTER 19: EQUALLY AT HOME IN PRIVATE AND PUBLIC SPHERES

[1]Chapter three of *Hearing God*, "Never Alone," gives a glimpse of the affection that Dallas had for London. In a touching story he tells of how he sat outside Westminster Cathedral within yards of my home, watching the world go by, and he reflects with tenderness on personal tragedy and the human condition. The words of Sting come to mind: "how fragile we are."

[2]Dallas Willard, *The Divine Conspiracy* (San Francisco: HarperCollins, 1998), pp. 61-62.

[3]Ibid., p. 68.

[4]Ibid., p. 69.

[5]Ibid., p. 78.

[6]N. T. Wright, *The New Testament and the People of God* (London: SPCK, 1992), pp. 41-42.

[7]Willard, *Divine Conspiracy*, p. 74.

[8]Ibid., p. 90.

[9]Nick Cohen, "Science Has Vanquished Religion, but Not Its Evils," *The Observer*, April 9, 2011, www.theguardian.com/commentisfree/2011 /apr/10/nick-cohen-religion-science.

[10]"There is," Dallas claims, "no field of expertise in human affairs where interaction with God is a part of the subject matter or practice that must be mastered in order to be judged competent. This is true of chemistry and public administration, but it is also true of education, nursing, police work and often, astonishingly, Christian ministry itself. . . . All of us live in such a world, for we live by our competencies. Our souls are, accordingly, soaked with secularity" (*Divine Conspiracy*, pp. 90-91).

[11]A most helpful essay by Darrell L. Bock, "Embracing Jesus in a First Century Context: What Can It Teach Us About Spiritual Commitment?" can be found in a special issue of *Journal of Spiritual Formation and Soul Care* 3, no. 2 (Fall 2010). Published by The Institute for Spiritual Formation at Biola University.

[12]Published in the UK as *Personal Religion, Public Reality?* (London: Hodder Faith, 1999).

[13]Evelyn Waugh, *Brideshead Revisited* (Boston: Little, Brown, 1946), pp. 85-86; Quoted in Willard, *Divine Conspiracy*, p. 92.

[14]Dallas Willard, *Knowing Christ Today* (New York: Harper One, 2009), p. 193.

[15]Ibid., p. 200.

[16]Ibid., p. 209.

[17]Ibid., p. 211.

DALLAS WILLARD CENTER
for Christian Spiritual Formation
WESTMONT COLLEGE

The Dallas Willard Center is dedicated to placing an enduring emphasis on the intellectual legacy of Dallas Willard, including his focus on the possibility and path to authentic spiritual and moral transformation. The Dallas Willard Center exists under the broader umbrella of the Martin Institute for Christianity and Culture.

Goals

The goals of the Martin Institute and Dallas Willard Center include:

- Creation of a new generation of individuals who will become thought leaders in articulating and experiencing an interactive relationship with Jesus Christ.

- Support the establishment of the field of Christian spiritual formation as a discipline of public knowledge that is open to research and pedagogy of the highest order.

The work of the Martin Institute and Dallas Willard Center is focused on three primary areas:

On-Campus Formation

The Martin Institute and Dallas Willard Center is working alongside the academic and student life departments at Westmont College to pilot a variety of spiritual formation programs and opportunities for students.

Research

The Martin Institute and Dallas Willard Center desires to support and engage in Christian spiritual formation research and writing efforts and to develop an online collection of materials accessible to researchers and other visitors. Early program initiatives include senior fellows program, annual book and research awards, and online research.

Resource Development

The Martin Institute and Dallas Willard Center desires to support new resource and program development in the area of Christian spiritual formation. Part of these efforts will include the cultivation of a network of professional contacts through hosting and participating in conferences, and collaborating with other organizations that share the goals of the Martin Institute and Dallas Willard Center.

formatio
TRADITION. EXPERIENCE.
TRANSFORMATION.

Formatio books from InterVarsity Press follow the rich tradition of the church in the journey of spiritual formation. These books are not merely about being informed, but about being transformed by Christ and conformed to his image. Formatio stands in InterVarsity Press's evangelical publishing tradition by integrating God's Word with spiritual practice and by prompting readers to move from inward change to outward witness. InterVarsity Press uses the chambered nautilus for Formatio, a symbol of spiritual formation because of its continual spiral journey outward as it moves from its center. We believe that each of us is made with a deep desire to be in God's presence. Formatio books help us to fulfill our deepest desires and to become our true selves in light of God's grace.